THE NEW IMMIGRANTS

Filipino Americans

Indian Americans

Jamaican Americans

Korean Americans

Mexican Americans

Ukrainian Americans

Vietnamese Americans

Philippines

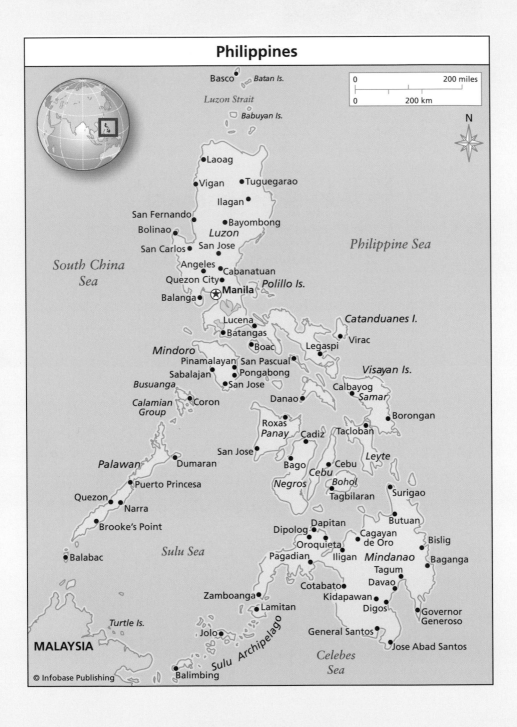

Basco ● · *Batan Is.*

Luzon Strait

0   200 miles

0   200 km

N

◌ *Babuyan Is.*

● Laoag

● Vigan   ● Tuguegarao

● Ilagan

San Fernando ●

Bolinao ●   ● Bayombong

Luzon

San Carlos ●   ● San Jose

Philippine Sea

South China Sea

● Angeles

Quezon City ●   ● Cabanatuan

Balanga ●   ⊛ **Manila**

Polillo Is.

● Lucena

● Batangas

● Boac

Catanduanes I.

● Virac

Legaspi ●

Mindoro

Pinamalayan ●   San Pascual ●

Sabalajan ●   ● Pongabong

Busuanga   ● San Jose

Visayan Is.

Calbayog ●

Danao ●   ● *Samar*

Calamian Group   ● Coron

● Borongan

Roxas ●

Panay   Cadiz ●   ● Tacloban

San Jose ●

Palawan   ● Dumaran

Bago ●   ● Cebu

Cebu

Leyte

● Puerto Princesa

Negros   *Bohol*

● Tagbilaran

● Surigao

Quezon ●

● Narra

Dapitan ●

● Butuan

● Brooke's Point

Dipolog ●   ● Dapitan

Cagayan de Oro ●

● Bislig

Sulu Sea

Oroquieta ●

Pagadian ●   Iligan ●   *Mindanao*   ● Baganga

● Balabac

Tagum ●

Cotabato ●   Davao ●

Zamboanga ●

● Lamitan

Kidapawan ●

● Digos

● Governor Generoso

Turtle Is.

Jolo ●

General Santos ●

Celebes Sea

MALAYSIA

Sulu Archipelago

● Jose Abad Santos

© Infobase Publishing

Balimbing ●

THE NEW IMMIGRANTS
FILIPINO
AMERICANS

Jon Sterngass

Series Editor: Robert D. Johnston
Associate Professor of History,
University of Illinois at Chicago

CHELSEA HOUSE
PUBLISHERS
An imprint of Infobase Publishing

Frontis: The Island nation of the Philippines is located in Southeast Asia. According to the 2000 U.S. census, 2.4 million Americans identified themselves as Filipino.

Filipino Americans

Chelsea House
An imprint of Infobase Publishing
132 West 31st Street
New York NY 10001

Library of Congress Cataloging-in-Publication Data
Sterngass, Jon.
  Filipino Americans / Jon Sterngass
      p. cm. — (The new immigrants)
  Includes bibliographical references and index.
  ISBN 0-7910-8791-3 (hardcover)
1. Filipino Americans—Juvenile literature. 2. Filipino Americans—Social conditions—Juvenile literature. 3. Immigrants—United States—History—Juvennile literature. 4. Immigrants—United States—Social conditions—Juvenile literature. 5. Philippines—Emigration and immigration—Juvenile literature. 6. United States—Emigration and immigration—Juvenile literature. I. Title. II. New immigrants (Chelsea House)
E184.F4S66 2006
973'.049921—dc22—dc22   2006015645

Chelsea House books are available at special discounts when purchased in bulk quantities for businesses, associations, institutions, or sales promotions. Please call our Special Sales Department in New York at (212) 967-8800 or (800) 322-8755.

You can find Chelsea House on the World Wide Web at
http://www.chelseahouse.com

Series design by Erika K. Arroyo
Cover design by Takeshi Takahashi

Printed in the United States of America
Bang EJB 10 9 8 7 6 5 4 3 2 1

This book is printed on acid-free paper.

All links and Web addresses were checked and verified to be correct at the time of publication. Because of the dynamic nature of the Web, some addresses and links may have changed since publication and may no longer be valid.

Contents

Introduction   6

1 Between Two Worlds   11

2 History of the Philippines   20

3 Manilamen, Pensionados, and Sakadas   39

4 New Opportunities   54

5 The Invisible Immigrants   64

6 Crossing Boundaries   76

7 Challenges for the Community   92

8 Politics and Activism   104

9 An Ongoing Story   118

Chronology   125

Timeline   126

Notes   130

Glossary   133

Bibliography   135

Further Reading   137

Index   139

Introduction

Robert D. Johnston

At the time of the publication of this series, there are few more pressing political issues in the country than immigration. Hundreds of thousands of immigrants are filling the streets of major U.S. cities to protect immigrant rights. And conflict in Congress has reached a boiling point, with members of the Senate and House fighting over the proper policy toward immigrants who have lived in the United States for years but who entered the country illegally.

Generally, Republicans and Democrats are split down partisan lines in a conflict of this sort. However, in this dispute, some otherwise conservative Republicans are taking a more liberal position on the immigration issue—precisely because of their own immigrant connections. For example, Pete Domenici, the longest-serving senator in the history of the state of New Mexico, recently told his colleagues about one of the most chilling days of his life.

In 1943, during World War II, the Federal Bureau of Investigation (FBI) set out to monitor U.S. citizens who had ties with Italy, Germany, and Japan. At the time, Domenici was 10 or 11 years old and living in Albuquerque, with his parents—Alda, the president of the local PTA, and Cherubino, an Italian-born grocer who already had become a U.S. citizen. Alda, who had arrived in the United States with her parents when she was three, thought she had her papers in order, but she found out otherwise when federal agents swept in and whisked her away—leaving young Pete in tears.

It turned out that Alda was an illegal immigrant. She was, however, clearly not a security threat, and the government released her on bond. Alda then quickly prepared the necessary paperwork and became a citizen. More than six decades later, her son decided to tell his influential colleagues Alda's story, because, he says, he wanted them to remember that "the sons and daughters of this century's illegal immigrants could end up in the Senate one day, too."[1]

Given the increasing ease of global travel, immigration is becoming a significant political issue throughout the world. Yet the United States remains in many ways the most receptive country toward immigrants that history has ever seen. The Statue of Liberty is still one of our nation's most important symbols.

A complex look at history, however, reveals that, despite the many success stories, there are many more sobering accounts like that of Pete Domenici. The United States has offered unparalleled opportunities to immigrants from Greece to Cuba, Thailand to Poland. Yet immigrants have consistently also suffered from persistent—and sometimes murderous—discrimination.

This series is designed to inform students of both the achievements and the hardships faced by some of the immigrant groups that have arrived in the United States since Congress passed the Immigration and Naturalization Services Act in 1965. The United States was built on the ingenuity and hard work of its nation's immigrants, and these new immigrants—primarily from Asia and

Latin America—have, over the last several decades, added their unique attributes to American culture.

Immigrants from the following countries are featured in THE NEW IMMIGRANTS series: India, Jamaica, Korea, Mexico, the Philippines, Ukraine, and Vietnam. Each book focuses on the present-day life of these ethnic groups—and not just in the United States, but in Canada as well. The books explore their culture, their success in various occupations, the economic hardships they face, and their political struggles. Yet all the authors in the series recognize that we cannot understand any of these groups without also coming to terms with their history—a history that involves not just their time in the United States, but also the lasting legacy of their homelands.

Mexican immigrants, along with their relatives and allies, have been the driving force behind the recent public defense of immigrant rights. Michael Schroeder explains how distinctive the situation of Mexican immigrants is, particularly given the fluid border between the United States and its southern neighbor. Indeed, not only is the border difficult to defend, but some Mexicans (and scholars) see it as an artificial barrier—the result of nineteenth-century imperialist conquest.

Vietnam is perhaps the one country outside of Mexico with the most visible recent connection to the history of the United States. One of the most significant consequences of our tragic war there was a flood of immigrants, most of whom had backed the losing side. Liz Sonneborn demonstrates how the historic conflicts over Communism in the Vietnamese homeland continue to play a role in the United States, more than three decades after the end of the "American" war.

In turn, Filipinos have also been forced out of their native land, but for them economic distress has been the primary cause. Jon Sterngass points out how immigration from the Philippines—as is the case with many Asian countries—reaches back much further in American history than is generally known, with the search for jobs a constant factor.

Koreans who have come to this country also demonstrate just how connected recent immigrants are to their "homelands" while forging a permanent new life in the United States. As Anne Soon Choi reveals, the history of twentieth-century Korea—due to Japanese occupation, division of the country after World War II, and the troubling power of dictators for much of postwar history—played a crucial role in shaping the culture of Korean Americans.

South Asians are, arguably, the greatest source of change in immigration to the United States since 1965. Padma Rangaswamy, an Indian-American scholar and activist, explores how the recent flow of Indians to this country has brought not only delicious food and colorful clothes, but also great technical expertise, as well as success in areas ranging from business to spelling bees.

Jamaican Americans are often best known for their music, as well as for other distinctive cultural traditions. Heather Horst and Andrew Garner show how these traditions can, in part, be traced to the complex and often bitter political rivalries within Jamaica—conflicts that continue to shape the lives of Jamaican immigrants.

Finally, the story of Ukrainian Americans helps us understand that even "white" immigrants suffered considerable hardship, and even discrimination in this land of opportunity. Still, the story that John Radzilowski portrays is largely one of achievement, particularly with the building of successful ethnic communities.

I would like to conclude by mentioning how proud I am to be the editor of this very important series. When I grew up in small-town Oregon during the 1970s, it was difficult to see that immigrants played much of a role in my "white bread" life. Even worse than that ignorance, however, were the lessons I learned from my relatives. They were, unfortunately, quite suspicious of all those they defined as "outsiders." Throughout his life, my grandfather believed that, the Japanese who immigrated to his rural valley in central Oregon were helping Japan during World War II by collecting scrap from gum wrappers to make weapons. My uncles, who were also fruit growers, were openly hostile toward the Mexican immigrants without whom they could not have harvested their apples and pears.

Fortunately, like so many other Americans, the great waves of immigration since 1965 have taught me to completely rethink my conception of America. I live in Chicago, a block from Devon Avenue, one of the primary magnets of Indian and Pakistani immigrations in this country (Padma Rangaswamy mentions Devon in her fine book in this series on Indian Americans). Conversely, when my family and I lived in Storm Lake, Iowa, in the early 1990s, immigrants from Laos, Mexico, and Somalia were also decisively reshaping the face of that small town. Throughout America, we live in a new country—one not without problems, but one that is incredibly exciting and vibrant. I hope that this series helps you appreciate even more one of the most special qualities of the American heritage.

Note

1. Rachel L. Swarns, "An Immigration Debate Framed by Family Ties," *New York Times,* April 4, 2006.

Robert D. Johnston
Chicago, Illinois
April 2006

1

Between Two Worlds

Rodney Salinas was born in 1975 in the city of Rosario, in the province of Cavite, on the island of Luzon in the Philippines. His mother was a nurse and his father was a 10-year veteran of the U.S. Navy. His family moved to New Jersey, in the United States, in the late 1970s.

As a teenager, Salinas found it difficult to preserve his *Filipino* identity. He said, "Thankfully, while I was attending college . . . I got involved with the school's Philippine Cultural Society. They taught me all the history, cultural dances and language that helped me get in touch with my Filipino heritage."[1]

Salinas's family still observes some Filipino customs. The men often wear the *barong tagalog*, which is the formal menswear of the Philippines. The children practice *pagmamano*, the Philippine custom of taking an older person's right hand and bringing it to their forehead as a sign of respect. *Tagalog* (the Philippines' national language) is still spoken in the house.

Salinas sometimes misses the Philippines. He said, "Most of all, I miss being with my extended family, the delicious food (especially fish), the television programming, and the beautiful countryside."

Like many *Filipino Americans*, however, Salinas also identifies himself with the United States and American culture. "While I am strongly Pinoy, I am also strongly American. Many Filipinos have this duality, which allows them to love both countries at the same time. I may be American on the outside, but my heart will forever be Filipino."[2]

Although no one person's account can speak for all of them, Rodney Salinas's story raises some very common issues. Filipinos who leave their homeland, like all immigrants, must

Filipino Americans take pride in preserving their culture through such activities as dance. Pictured here are dancers from Ramon Obusan's Ballet Folklorico De Filipinas performing "Ragragsakan." The performance was part of a yearlong celebration in Hawaii marking the centennial of Filipino immigration to the United States in 2006.

decide who they are, how much of their past they wish to keep, and how much allegiance they owe the nation they have left behind.

THE FILIPINO DIASPORA

People who live in the Philippines, whether male or female, are called *Filipinos*. Women are sometimes called *Filipinas*. A *Filipino American* is a Filipino or Filipina who has come to live in the United States. The term *Filipino American* is often shortened to *Pinoy*. The origin of the name is uncertain, although it first became popular in the 1920s. Residents of the Philippines later adopted the term *Pinoy* to describe themselves. People sometimes use Pinoy to mean not just being a Filipino by birth but also being a Filipino in thought, deed, and spirit.

The word *diaspora* comes from the Greek word meaning "dispersion." A diaspora is the migration or scattering of people from their original homeland, often because of conquest, slavery, or poverty. Filipinos have been following their dreams of a better life in foreign lands for centuries, although a large movement of Filipino workers to other countries did not begin until the mid-1970s. At that time, the Philippine government began to encourage its citizens to find work overseas. Since then, the Philippines has exported workers in order to reduce the high unemployment in that country.

In the early 2000s, almost a million Filipinos left the country every year to live or work in more than 100 countries around the world. Most of them were looking for temporary, higher paying jobs. A growing number, however, emigrated from the Philippines for good. They no longer wanted to live in a country where more than half the population lived on $3 a day or less.

By 2005, an estimated 8 million Filipino workers were scattered across the globe; these included about 3.1 million immigrants and their families, 3.6 million documented overseas Filipino workers, and 1.3 million undocumented overseas Filipino workers. About 10 percent of the population of the Philippines lives outside the country. More than 2 million people of Filipino descent live in the United States and another 1.5 million in the Middle East. There are also large communities in Japan, Hong Kong, and Taiwan. One anthropologist noted, "We are now several decades into the Filipino diaspora with Filipinos now living in all corners of the world."[3]

MODERN-DAY HEROES

Overseas Filipino workers and immigrants have helped prop up the shaky Philippine economy. In the early 2000s, Filipinos who live abroad sent home about $8 billion annually. This money from overseas is called a *remittance*. Remittances to the Philippines from workers overseas equaled about 20 percent of exports. Remittances have become one of the nation's most important ways of getting foreign currency that the country would have trouble obtaining in any other way. The Philippines is the third-largest recipient of remittances in the world, after Mexico and India. This money has improved the standard of living throughout the Philippines.

In addition to remittances, many Filipino Americans send *balikbayan boxes*, stuffed with goods for relatives, to different parts of the Philippines. These boxes may contain canned goods, new and old clothes, electronics, and anything else that may be of use to Filipino Americans' relatives back home.

The government of the Philippines counts on the remittances. In 2004, the foreign affairs secretary of the Philippines told an audience of Filipino Americans in New York City that they were "modern-day heroes," blazing "a trail of professional and economic success in almost every nook and cranny of the globe." He asked them to continue to send money home, so that they could say, "'Yes, while I was living the American dream, I also helped our motherland stay the economic course.'"[4]

THE FILIPINO WAY

Culture is the learned behaviors of a group of people. A country's history helps determine its culture. When Filipinos move to more modernized countries such as the United States, they often have trouble holding onto the traditional Filipino way of

First-Person Account

ALAN ZOBEL

Alan Zobel was a Manila newspaper reporter who protested against the Ferdinand Marcos regime and left the Philippines in 1979. He and his wife settled in New York and after struggling to make a living for a number of years, Zobel eventually found work as a writer. He remembered,

> I left because I had to. My wife was threatened as well as myself. It wasn't easy at first. I drove a cab for five years. I tried to write articles but all I knew was Philippine politics, and nobody cared about that then. My wife got a job as a maid in a hotel. My wife and I were watching the news when we saw that Benigno Aquino had been assassinated.
>
> Together, we wept.
>
> After that, there was a flurry of interest in Philippine politics, and I got some work as a researcher on a news magazine. That led to a writing job. I was pretty settled in New York when Corazon Aquino was elected, and my wife and I discussed whether we should go back. We decided to stay because things were so uncertain there, and because my wife had just entered a university. . . . I write about politics and human rights, important issues that need to be examined. I don't want to write the truth and have to look over my shoulder.[*]

[*] Alexandra Bandon, *Filipino Americans* (New York: New Discovery Books, 1993), 29.

life. It is not so much a matter of wearing Filipino clothes or cooking Filipino meals. Filipinos have a style that is not so easily transplanted to the United States.

For example, Filipino culture has several ways of maintaining relationships that are quite different from the American style. Like many Asians, Filipinos emphasize smooth social interaction between people, known in the Tagalog language as *pakikisama.* This often means going along with the decisions of a group even if one disagrees, or acting pleasantly even if angry.

Pride and self-esteem are extremely important in Filipino culture. Filipinos often avoid sensitive topics in order to prevent misunderstandings, criticisms, or fights. They are extremely careful about "losing face"; an apology will not always solve the situation if someone is offended. Therefore, it is important in Filipino culture to avoid upsetting anyone or to give an outright negative answer to a question. Pakikisama helps Filipinos get along as a group and helps them to avoid causing anyone shame or embarassment.

Another important concept in Filipino culture that is hard for immigrants to retain is *bayanihan,* which means "cooperative work." Filipinos often help each other in both large and small matters. Helping another person leads to *utang na loob,* which means a "debt of gratitude." As in most traditional cultures, if someone does a favor for another person, that person is obligated to return the favor at some future time. The payment depends on a person's ability to pay and does not necessarily have to be in material form. Filipinos are honored to be asked a favor, and favors are never forgotten.

Americans often find this type of Filipino social interaction confusing. In the United States, the individual is more important than the group. Although not "losing face" is important to Americans, society in the United States is much more confrontational and competitive. "Getting along" does not give a person as much status in America as "getting ahead."

Important favors are written down as legal contracts in the United States; if a favor is not in writing, it may or may not be repaid.

THE IMPORTANCE OF FAMILY

Changes in family relations are also upsetting to Filipino immigrants to America. In the United States, family groups are small, usually only consisting of parents and children. Easy geographical mobility means families are often scattered across the continent or even the world.

In the Philippines, however, as in most traditional societies, the extended family is central to life and culture. *Lolos* (grandfathers), *lolas* (grandmothers), uncles, aunts, cousins, and even godparents all play a much larger role in Filipino society than in American culture. Filipinos usually live near and have personal relationships with many people in their extended families. They love to celebrate with families, extended families, and friends. Some families host as many as a dozen celebrations each year, including baptisms, birthdays, holidays, and weddings. These celebrations often grow into major parties.

In Filipino culture, family members assume responsibility for each other. Family obligations are more important than a person's responsibility to the government, their duty to an employer, and especially their own personal preference. Utang na loob is the grease that makes Filipino family life run smoothly.

In a Filipino home, *ama* (the father), as the oldest male, is rarely questioned. *Ina* (the mother) regulates the household, including the family budget. In traditional Filipino culture, children have very little independence. They are supposed to respect their elders and defer to their experience and wisdom. All of this is quite different from the youth-centered culture that Filipino Americans encounter when they move to the United States.

In traditional Filipino culture, nurturing relationships with the extended family are very important. However, in the United States, many Filipino families follow the traditional nuclear model, which consists of a husband and wife and their children. Here, a father plays with his two children in Santa Barbara, California.

Filipino society, like many traditional societies, emphasizes family closeness, respect for elders, communal life, and utang na loob. In the United States, however, many Americans focus on independence, youth, individualism, and materialism. It is difficult for Filipinos in the United States to hold onto the values they associate with their homeland. Their children, often born in America, are sometimes contemptuous of "old-fashioned" ways. They want to *assimilate*, or fit into their new environment. They want to avoid standing out from their peers!

• Study Questions •

1. What are some Filipino customs that Rodney Salinas has tried to keep in the United States?
   ....
2. Approximately how many Filipinos lived outside the Philippines in 2005?
   ....
3. When did the Filipino diaspora begin?
   ....
4. Why did Filipinos want to leave the Philippines?
   ....
5. What are remittances and why are they important?
   ....
6. Give one example of how the "Filipino way" is different from the "American way."
   ....

2

History of the Philippines

The nation known as the Philippines is made up of hundreds of islands in the southwest Pacific Ocean. The country stretches 1,152 miles (1,855 kilometers) from north to south and 688 miles (1,108 kilometers) from east to west. The Philippines is bounded by the Philippine Sea on the east, the Celebes Sea on the south, and the South China Sea on the west. Although about 400 of the islands are inhabited, more than 90 percent of the population lives on the 11 largest islands: Luzon, Mindanao, Samar, Negros, Palawan, Panay, Mindoro, Leyte, Cebu, Bohol, and Masbate. If all the islands of the Philippines were combined, they would be about the size of the state of Arizona.

The Philippines has a large and growing population. According to the 2000 U.S. census, about 77 million Filipinos live in that country, making it the world's twelfth-most populated nation. This amazing growth from a mere 20 million around 1950 has led to severe economic problems. Between one-fourth and one-half of the Philippine population lives in poverty. Unemployment is consistently above 10 percent.

Philippine Population (in millions)*	
1948	19
1960	27
1970	37
1980	48
1990	61
2000	77
2006	89 (estimated)

*Source: http://www.census.gov.ph

The capital of the Philippines is Manila, on the great bay of Luzon. Manila is also the largest city in the country and its main port. Other important cities are Quezon City on Luzon, Cebu on Cebu Island, Iloilo on Panay, Davao and Zamboanga on Mindanao, and Jolo on Jolo Island.

The islands that make up the Philippines were mostly formed by volcanoes. The larger islands often have narrow coastal plains and mountain ranges in the middle. Most people live in the hot and humid lowland areas. The warm tropical climate, heavy rainfall, and fertile volcanic soil have helped Filipino farmers. Rice, corn, and coconuts make up about 80 percent of all cropland. Parts of the Philippines still have dense forests, and mahogany is an important export.

In appearance and in culture, the Filipino people are a blend of Asian, European, and American. Most of the people of the Philippines claim Malay ethnicity, because their ancestors came from the Malayan archipelago in Asia. There is much mixing of different heritages, however—a result of a long history of

The warm tropical climate of the Philippines is conducive to growing the country's most important crop—rice. A staple crop for Filipinos, rice makes up approximately 40 percent of their caloric intake. Pictured here are the rice terraces of the Cordillera region, which have been declared a World Heritage site by the United Nations Educational, Scientific, and Cultural Organization (UNESCO).

Spanish and American colonial rule, as well as the visits of Chinese and Arab merchants and traders.

The culture of the Philippines is different from most of its neighbors in the Pacific and Southeast Asia—people from opposite sides of the world have come to the country and left their mark. Because Catholic Spain ruled the islands for more than 300 years, Filipinos make up one of the largest Christian groups in Asia. More than four out of every five Filipinos is a Roman Catholic. Another 10 percent are Muslims, who live mostly in the south, especially on Mindanao.

About eight major languages, with more than 80 dialects, are spoken in the Philippines. Since 1987, the official national language has been Filipino, a form of Tagalog. Many Filipinos also speak English, because the nation was a *colony* of the United States from 1899 to 1946. The ability of Filipinos to speak English has been beneficial in today's world, where English has become the language of business, science, and culture.

Most industry on the Philippines is based near Manila. The country's most important exports are electronics and telecommunications equipment, lumber, machinery, clothing, coconut products, copper, chemicals, and sugar. Philippine businesses send their products mostly to the United States and Japan.

EARLY HISTORY

People have lived on the Philippines for at least 250,000 years. Some migrants probably came during the ice ages. At that time, the water level of the Pacific Ocean was much lower than today and people could reach the Philippines by land. When the last ice age ended about 10,000 years ago, rising waters caused by the melting of glaciers submerged the land bridges linking the Philippines to Asia. The first seafaring migrants to the Philippine Islands were probably Indonesians, who arrived about 6,000 years ago.

Malay people began arriving about 1500 B.C. They are distinguished physically by their brown skin, medium height, and straight black hair. Malays are the ancestors of more than one-third of Filipinos today. Much of Filipino traditional culture, including the Tagalog language, has Malay roots. Malays introduced iron, glass, the art of weaving, and the use of the water buffalo as the traditional draft animal of the Philippines.

Other nearby kingdoms and peoples have also influenced the Philippines. From about A.D. 500 to 1100, the Buddhist empire of Sri Vijaya on Sumatra shaped Filipino culture. In the 1300s, the Philippines came under the influence of the Hindu kingdom of Majapahit, centered in Java. During China's Ming Dynasty (1368–1644), Chinese trading outposts sprang up throughout the Philippines. Filipinos traded pearls, mats, shells, and wax for Chinese silks and porcelains. At about the same time, Arab traders from Malay and Borneo spread Islam into the Sulu Archipelago, Mindanao, and even as far as Luzon.

SPANISH CONTROL

In 1521, a Spanish expedition of five ships led by explorer Ferdinand Magellan landed in the Philippines. These were the first European visitors. Like Christopher Columbus some 30 years earlier, Ferdinand Magellan was seeking a shorter westward route to the Spice Islands (the Moluccas) and the riches of China and India. Lapu Lapu, a native chief who rebelled against Spanish rule, killed Magellan and many of his men in a fierce battle. A single ship from Magellan's expedition, however, completed the three-year voyage, to become the first ship to sail around the world.

After Magellan's voyage, the Spanish continued to cross the Pacific searching for trade routes to Asia. In 1543, on one of these voyages, a Spanish captain named the Philippine Islands after the prince of Spain, who would one day become King Philip II. Spanish rule of the Philippines began in 1565. In 1571, the Spanish established the city of Manila. For the next three centuries, the Spanish ruled the Philippines. They united the scattered islands into a single country and introduced schools and some organization. Spanish missionaries converted practically the entire population to Christianity. Unfortunately, the Spanish exploited the Philippines to benefit Spain. Spanish missionaries ran great plantations worked by the natives, whom the Spanish treated almost like slaves. The central Spanish government in Manila was very corrupt. Spanish authorities often had to put down uprisings by the Filipinos, who resented Spanish rule.

By 1600, Manila had become a flourishing center of trade. Spanish ships, known as galleons, carried gold, silk, spices, and gems between Asia and the Philippines and then the Philippines and the Spanish colony of Mexico. The Philippines themselves did export some tobacco, sugarcane, and abacá (used to make rope). It was the location of the islands, however, more than their products, that made them valuable.

The Philippines remained a Spanish colony from 1565 to 1898. This is nearly 300 years longer than it was an American colony (1899–1946). Spain influenced the Philippine language, literature, food, architecture, and other aspects of custom and culture. Most Filipinos have Spanish surnames, and many have Spanish ancestors. In a way, Filipinos are as Hispanic as people from Chile or Cuba.

FILIPINOS REVOLT AGAINST SPAIN

Many Filipinos resented Spanish rule. They felt the Spanish government was prejudiced against native Filipinos and was robbing the country of its wealth. In the late 1800s, Filipinos began to talk about independence.

José Rizal (1861–1896), a doctor, poet, and writer, worked to empower the people of the Philippines. Rizal was born in the Philippines and lived in Europe for five years while he studied medicine. In 1887, he attacked corruption in the Spanish administration and the religious orders in the Philippines in his first novel, *Noli Me Tangere* (translated as *Touch Me Not*). Later that year, as a result of his outspokenness, Spanish officials forced Rizal to leave the Philippines. Rizal lived in exile in China, Japan, the United States, England, and France, before establishing himself as a doctor in Hong Kong.

Rizal believed in changing society by peaceful means. From Hong Kong, Rizal established the Filipino League, an organization dedicated to land redistribution and peaceful reform on the islands. Rizal returned to Manila in 1892, where the Spanish arrested him as a revolutionary and banished him to Mindanao. In 1896, the Katipunan, a large patriotic secret society, began a Filipino revolt against Spain. The Spanish wrongly accused Rizal of starting the fighting and executed him. Rizal was only 35 years old. The day of his execution, December 30, is a national holiday in the Philippines.

Rizal's execution caused a full-scale rebellion against Spanish rule. Emilio Aguinaldo, a Filipino leader, freed several towns south of Manila and declared the Philippines an independent nation. A short-lived peace was made with Spain, but a new revolution was about to begin when the Spanish-American War broke out in 1898.

THE SPANISH-AMERICAN WAR

The Spanish-American War began when the United States supported the independence movement in the Spanish colony of Cuba in the Caribbean. The U.S. government, however, had a larger strategy. As soon as the war began, George Dewey, commander of the United States Asiatic Squadron, located in Hong Kong, left the coast of China and steamed toward the Philippines. He entered Manila Bay on the night of April 30, 1898. At daybreak, he opened fire on the Spanish fleet from a distance of 5,000 yards (4,572 meters). The guns of Dewey's ships had much greater range than those of the Spanish fleet, so the American ships could fire without fear of retaliation. When the smoke had cleared, all 10 Spanish ships had been destroyed.

After the United States won this confrontation, called the Battle of Manila Bay, Dewey supplied Aguinaldo with arms and urged him to rally the Filipinos against the Spanish. By the time American land forces arrived, the Filipinos had taken almost the entire island of Luzon and surrounded the old walled city of Manila. Dewey then asked for troops to take and hold Manila. U.S. President William McKinley took the fateful step of sending 11,000 soldiers. On August 13, 1898, these forces, joined by Filipino soldiers under Aguinaldo, captured the Philippine capital.

The fall of Manila completely changed the character of the Spanish-American War. The liberation of the Philippines had not originally been a war aim of the United States. The American people thought they were fighting for Cuban

Filipino patriot José Rizal believed in creating an independent Philippines through nonviolent protest. In 1887, the Spanish government exiled him after he published *Noli Me Tangere* (*Touch Me Not*), which supported social change in the Philippines. The Spanish executed Rizal in 1896 for his perceived role as a revolutionary, but the date of his execution—December 30—is celebrated as a national holiday in the Philippines.

independence. They knew almost nothing about the Philippine Islands. Yet now they would have to decide what to do with them.

THE UNITED STATES TAKES OVER

After quickly defeating the Spanish in Cuba, in 1898, the United States and Spain drew up the Treaty of Paris. To the shock of the Filipinos, the treaty did not give them their independence. Instead, it simply transferred the islands to the United States.

The treaty aroused opposition even in the United States, where many people did not want to own the Philippines. Well-known Americans, such as industrialist Andrew Carnegie, writer Mark Twain, social worker Jane Addams, and former presidents Grover Cleveland and Benjamin Harrison fought against the treaty. Anti-imperialists argued that by imposing its power on others, the United States violated its beliefs in self-determination and democracy. They believed annexing the Philippines would lead to greater presidential power, an expensive and unnecessary standing army, entangling foreign alliances, and large taxes. Anti-imperialists also used racial arguments. Former U.S. Senator Carl Schurz complained that acquiring the Philippines would greatly aggravate the nation's serious racial problems. For Schurz, the thought of Malays and Tagalogs participating in "our government is so alarming that you instinctively pause before taking the step."[5] Many worried that white Southerners would oppose any policy that might add nonwhites to the United States.

In 1899, however, the U.S. Senate approved the Treaty of Paris by a two-vote margin. An amendment that promised independence as soon as the Filipinos formed a stable government was defeated by one vote. The Philippines was now part of the United States' colonial empire.

Filipinos were not about to see their dreams of independence crushed so easily by another colonial power. In 1899, Aguinaldo once again proclaimed an independent Philippine Republic and led a new revolt, this time against American rule. The revolt eventually turned into a savage guerrilla war that did not end until the capture of Aguinaldo in 1901.

The Philippine-American War cost far more money and took far more lives than the Spanish-American War. More than

60,000 U.S. troops were needed to put down the Filipino independence movement. Americans suffered 4,200 deaths, 10 times more than the number sustained in the Spanish-American War. Filipino casualty numbers are still disputed and very controversial; estimates range from 40,000 to 200,000 killed, out of a population of about 7 million.

While a colony, the Philippines received the benefit of American-built roads and schools. Public health and sanitation were greatly improved. American corporations controlled the Philippine economy, however. They did nothing to redistribute the land fairly. Like most colonies, the Philippines was mostly used by the United States for the benefit of Americans.

THE JAPANESE ATTACK THE PHILIPPINES

By the 1930s, many U.S. citizens had decided that the Philippines were more trouble than they were worth. The U.S. economy had collapsed in the 1930s, the decade of the Great Depression. Americans were more worried about jobs than foreign affairs. At the same time, in 1931, Japan began expanding into Asia by invading China. Americans feared that owning the Philippines would somehow draw the United States into a war with Japan.

As a result, the U.S. Congress passed the Tydings-McDuffie Act of 1934. This law provided for complete independence for the Philippines after 10 years of self-government under American rule. In 1936, the Philippines became a self-governing "commonwealth." To defend against possible Japanese attack, the United States sent General Douglas MacArthur to the islands as a military adviser in 1935. The following year, he supervised the creation of the Philippine Army.

World War II came suddenly to the United States on December 7, 1941, when, without warning, Japan attacked the U.S. Navy at Pearl Harbor, Hawaii. Even after receiving word of Pearl Harbor, MacArthur did not prepare for an attack, and the U.S. Air Force left its B-17s wing-to-wing on the Clark

Field runways. A full 10 hours after the attack on Pearl Harbor, while U.S. pilots ate lunch, a large force of Japanese bombers destroyed the U.S. Air Force on the ground. This allowed the Japanese to control the sky over the Philippines and removed one of the last effective fighting forces that might have opposed their move into Southeast Asia.

Japanese troops invaded the Philippines on December 22 at Lingayen Gulf and easily defeated the U.S. and Filipino soldiers. The Japanese conquered Manila on January 2, 1942. General MacArthur's scattered defending forces (about 80,000 troops, four-fifths of them Filipinos) retreated to the Bataan Peninsula and Corregidor Island. These strategic positions guarded the entrance to Manila Bay. The Americans and Filipinos tried to hold out until the arrival of reinforcements, but no reinforcements came. MacArthur left for Australia on March 11, 1942, famously announcing, "I shall return." The words, however, seemed like a hollow promise at the time. The Japanese now controlled Malaya, Singapore, Hong Kong, the Dutch East Indies, Burma, Guam, and Wake Island.

The besieged U.S.–Filipino Army on Bataan finally crumbled on April 9, and the 11,000 men on Corregidor surrendered on May 6. The Japanese forced 70,000 captured Philippine and American soldiers to march to prisoner-of-war camps. The conditions were terrible, and almost 20,000 men, most of them Filipinos, died on what became known as the Bataan Death March. Many individual soldiers in the Philippines, however, refused to surrender. Guerrilla resistance continued throughout the Japanese occupation.

THE DEFEAT OF THE JAPANESE

As Japan expanded its holdings in Asia, the Japanese preached that Asians, and not European countries or the United States, should govern Asia. The Japanese tried to win Filipino loyalty by establishing a "Philippine Republic." The slogan "Asia for Asians," however, turned out to mean "Asia for the Japanese."

Filipinos suffered greatly from the brutal Japanese occupation, and the Japanese-supported "puppet" government gained little support. During World War II, more than 200,000 Filipinos fought in defense of the United States against the Japanese in the Pacific. By the end of the war, more than 100,000 Filipinos had been killed, including more than 80,000 civilians.

Beginning in 1943, the United States began to turn back the Japanese tide in the Pacific. On October 20, 1944, liberation forces under MacArthur surprised the Japanese by landing at Leyte, in the heart of the Philippine Islands. In the week after the landing, the United States and Japan fought the largest naval battle in history. This Battle of Leyte Gulf, also known as the second battle of the Philippine Sea, was a tremendous American victory. The Japanese fleet was destroyed as a fighting force. The Americans invaded Luzon and took Manila in February 1945. On July 5, 1945, MacArthur announced, "All the Philippines are now liberated."

THE REPUBLIC OF THE PHILIPPINES

The Philippines faced enormous problems after World War II. Manila lay in ruins, and the economy had been destroyed. For many, the jobs and homes they had before the war were gone completely. The country was torn by political warfare and guerrilla violence. As promised, though, the United States granted the Philippines its independence on July 4, 1946. Manuel Roxas became the first president of the independent Republic of the Philippines. The political situation in the world had changed, however. The United States and the Soviet Union were embroiled in the Cold War, and the United States was now very interested in controlling events in Asia. U.S. foreign policymakers insisted that even though the Philippines was independent, it should follow American policy. The island's constitution was amended to give American businesses and corporations special rights to the natural resources of the Philippines. In 1947, the Philippines and the United States signed a military assistance pact.

To make sure the Philippines remained loyal, the United States demanded that the Philippines give America a 99-year lease on certain military, naval, and air bases. Subic Bay, a U.S. Navy base on the west coast of Luzon, about 60 miles (100 kilometers) northwest of Manila Bay, became one of the largest U.S. military bases in Asia. Clark Air Base, about 40 miles (60 kilometers) northwest of Manila, was the largest overseas U.S. military base in the world. At its peak, Clark had a population of 15,000. These bases remained a stronghold of American power in the Philippines and in Asia from the end of World War II until 1992. During the United States' war in Vietnam (1965–1973), most supplies were shipped to U.S. forces in Vietnam through American military bases in the Philippines.

Many Filipinos objected to U.S. military bases on independent Filipino soil. In 1956, the United States recognized that the Philippine government had full control over Clark and Subic Bay. Tensions continued for the next 35 years, however. The United States wanted Philippine support in order to project American power in Asia. In order to do this, the United States was willing to support a dictator, as long as he was pro-American.

THE MARCOS ERA

The Philippines experienced a good deal of chaos in the late 1960s. There were uprisings by poor Filipinos against landowners on Luzon, civil war on Mindanao between Muslims and Christians, assassinations of elected officials, and acts of terror against voters. Against this background, Ferdinand Marcos, a senator from the Ilocos del Norte Province, won the presidency in the 1965 elections and was reelected in 1969.

President Marcos blamed the unrest on Filipinos who wanted to overthrow his government. Marcos declared *martial law* in 1972. Martial law places the military, instead of the civilian government and the police, in complete control of a country. Marcos suspended the Philippine Congress and replaced the nation's constitution with a new one that gave more power to the president. For the next 10 years, Marcos ran the Philippines as a dictator. He became increasingly corrupt—granting jobs, contracts, and favors to his friends and relatives. The Philippine economy declined, and educated Filipinos began leaving the country in large numbers. No one who spoke out against the Marcos government was safe. Under martial law, the president controlled the press, radio, and television, and arrested opposition leaders.

Many Filipinos thought that Marcos remained in power only through the influence and support of the United States. They especially did not like the fact that Marcos supported the American war in Vietnam. Throughout the 1970s, poverty and government corruption increased. Martial law remained in force until 1981.

THE 1986 EDSA REVOLUTION

Mariá Corazón "Cory" Sumulong Cojuangco was born in 1933 in Manila into one of the richest families in the Philippines. She studied at Catholic schools in Philadelphia, Pennsylvania, graduated from Mount St. Vincent College in New York, and returned to the Philippines to study law. In 1955, Cory married Benigno Aquino, Jr., who had just been elected mayor of Concepción at age 22. They had five children together. He rose to be governor and senator. Then, under the Marcos regime, Benigno Aquino was arrested, sentenced to death, and exiled. Cory Aquino went with him into exile to the United States in 1980.

In August 1983, Aquino returned to the Philippines. To the shock of the world, he was assassinated as he was leaving his plane at Manila Airport. Aquino's murder, and the likelihood that members of Marcos's government were involved, caused a powerful wave of opposition to Marcos. Mass demonstrations followed, and opposition newspapers blossomed.

International criticism forced Marcos to hold a presidential election in 1986. Cory Aquino decided to run against Marcos.

After the election, her supporters claimed that Marcos tried to steal the election through fraud and violence. Both the Philippine Army and the U.S. government refused to support Marcos any longer. Marcos fled the Philippines and moved to the United States in 1986. He died in exile in Hawaii in 1989.

The Philippine Revolution of 1986 is sometimes known as the People Power Revolution or the *EDSA Revolution.* EDSA stands for Epifanio de los Santos Avenue, the main highway in Manila. It was there that more than a million Filipinos assembled in a nonviolent mass demonstration against Marcos for four days.

THE PHILIPPINES AFTER MARCOS

Unfortunately, the situation in the Philippines improved only slightly after the EDSA Revolution. Cory Aquino's government faced difficult political and economic problems. The population boom led to low wages for workers and high unemployment. Land reform was a constant problem, because rich farmers or large corporations still controlled most of the best Filipino farmland. The Philippine Army continued to meddle in politics and tried to overthrow the government. Several natural disasters, including the eruption of Mount Pinatubo on Luzon and a series of severe typhoons and earthquakes, hurt the country's economy. Muslims in the south demanded greater independence and fought the government on and off from 1987 through 2005.

One success, however, was the removal of the U.S. bases on Philippine soil. In 1991, the Philippine Senate refused to renew the lease for Clark Air Base and Subic Bay Naval Base. After nearby Mount Pinatubo erupted and covered the area around the bases with ash, the U.S. government removed its troops, and the bases were closed in 1992.

Corazón Aquino decided not to run for president again, and her army chief of staff, Fidel Ramos, succeeded her in 1992. Then, Joseph Marcelo Estrada, a former movie actor, was elected president in 1998. Estrada was a favorite among the poor people of the Philippines. He promised to help the poor and develop the country's agriculture.

No sooner was Estrada elected president, however, than his opponents accused him of corruption and criminal activity. In November 2000, the Philippine House of Representatives impeached Estrada for accepting millions of dollars in payoffs from illegal gambling operations. Estrada maintained the support of the Philippines' poor, but almost all important political, business, and church leaders in the country called for him to resign. A million Filipinos met at the EDSA shrine to protest against President Estrada, after the Senate of the Philippines refused to convict him. Tremendous confusion resulted and the country was on the verge of civil war.

In January 2001, the Philippine Army, seeing the chaos in the country, withdrew its support for the president and transferred its allegiance to the vice president, Gloria Macapagal-Arroyo. Without military support, Estrada's government quickly fell. Most nations around the world recognized Arroyo as the new president, as did Philippine government officials, the military, and the national police. This change in government is sometimes known as EDSA II, although a major difference from EDSA I was that Estrada was a democratically elected leader and not a dictator.

THE CONTINUING PROBLEM OF CORRUPTION

In December 2002, Macapagal-Arroyo declared that she would not run in the 2004 elections. Unfortunately, she changed her mind 10 months later. Her main opponent was Fernando Poe, another movie actor and a supporter of Joseph Estrada. In the Philippine presidential election of May 2004, Macapagal-Arroyo successfully won a full six-year term by defeating Poe by a margin of just over one million votes. As usual, violence and fraud accompanied the voting. The next year, the president's opponents claimed there was strong evidence that

Gloria Macapagal-Arroyo, pictured here with former presidents Corazón Aquino (left) and Fidel Ramos (right), is the second female president of the Philippines and was reelected for a second term in 2004. Here, Macapagal-Arroyo, Aquino, and Ramos celebrate the 18th anniversary of the People Power Revolution, which ousted Filipino dictator Ferdinand Marcos in 1986.

Macapagal-Arroyo had rigged the 2004 election. They claimed government officials had used their positions to commit election fraud and then tried to cover it up. The government has denied some of the allegations and challenged others in court.

The controversy over the election of 2004 underlines the Philippines' reputation for political corruption and bribery. The concept of utang na loob (repaying a debt of gratitude) has had enormous influence on politics in the Philippines. Politics is very personal in the Philippines. Repaying favors has often led to dishonesty, illegal payoffs, or hiring friends and relatives for government jobs whether or not they are competent.

This has gone on so long that Filipinos seem to no longer care if their politicians cheat during elections. After the election of 2004, one newspaper commented, "There were allegations of mass fraud, violence, and vote buying. Philippine politics and elections, for that matter, have always had the usual ingredients of guns, goons, and gold. So what else is new?" Filipinos usually doubt their leaders have been elected fairly, especially in close elections. The lack of political stability has become a major reason for the economic instability, and the combination has led many Filipinos to leave their homeland for a better life or the chance to make more money elsewhere.

• Study Questions •

1. Where are the Philippine Islands?
   ....

2. For how long was the Philippines a Spanish colony?
   ....

3. For how long was the Philippines an American colony?
   ....

4. Who was José Rizal?
   ....

(continues on next page)

(continued from previous page)

5. What was the result of the Philippine-American War?
   ....

6. What was the Bataan Death March?
   ....

7. When did the Philippines become independent?
   ....

8. Why did the United States establish military bases in the Philippines?
   ....

9. Who was Ferdinand Marcos?
   ....

10. What was the EDSA Revolution?
   ....

3

Manilamen, Pensionados, and Sakadas

Although Filipinos did not come to the United States in large numbers until the 1900s, a few came to North America long before that. During the 1500s, ships from Spain traveled between the Spanish colonies of the Philippines and Mexico. They traded the silks and gems of Asia for silver from America. On the way from Manila to the Mexican port of Acapulco, the ships often stopped on the California coast. (California belonged to Spain until 1821.)

Because the captains treated the sailors so badly, there was always a shortage of sailors to work on the Spanish ships. Many would desert the ship as soon as it reached the shores of a new land. The Spanish captains knew that Filipinos were excellent sailors and often forced them to serve on Spanish ships. This is how the first Filipinos, known as "Luzon Indians," arrived in North America. In 1587, Filipinos onboard a Manila-built galleon landed in Morro Bay, near present-day San Luis Obispo, California.

By the late 1700s, a line of Spanish settlements stretched between what is today San Francisco and San Diego, California. Although it is not known for sure, probably some of the thousands of Filipinos who served as sailors on Spanish ships "jumped ship" in Acapulco and stayed on in Mexico and California. One Filipino known to have lived in Mexico was Antonio Miranda Rodriguez. In 1781, the Spanish government of Mexico chose him to be a member of the first group of settlers (*pobladors*) to establish the city of Los Angeles, California.

Filipinos did not establish permanent settlements in North America until 1763, however. At that time, Filipino sailors known as *Manilamen* left their Spanish ships in Mexico and crossed the Gulf of Mexico to southern Louisiana. In Barataria Bay, they established several Philippine-style fishing villages. In time, a few hundred settled in the bayous and swamps outside New Orleans. They founded Filipino settlements such as St. Malo, in Bernard Parish, and Leon Rojas, Bayou Cholas, and Bassa Bassa, in Jefferson Parish.

These communities prospered during the 1800s. The Manilamen of Louisiana introduced the idea of sun-drying Louisiana shrimp so that the dried shrimp could be exported. The Filipinos intermarried with Spanish and French immigrants to Louisiana. Their descendants are sometimes called "Filipino Creoles" or "Filipino Cajuns." By the early 1900s, more than 2,000 people of Filipino ancestry lived in the New Orleans area.

PENSIONADOS AND STUDENTS

During the first 40 years of U.S. control over the Philippines, about 150,000 Filipinos immigrated to the United States. In that period, Filipinos in the United States had a peculiar status. Because the Philippines was an American territory, the U.S. government declared that Filipinos were "nationals," rather than "aliens," such as immigrants from Japan and China. They could enter the United States without restrictions. Their "national" status meant they were not eligible for U.S. citizenship, a choice that was open to "alien" immigrants, however.

The first group of Filipinos came to America to seek an education and then return home. In 1903, the U.S. government passed the Pensionado Act. This law provided government scholarships (or pensions) for Filipino students to study in the United States. Congress hoped that these American-educated Filipinos would eventually provide pro-American leadership in the Philippines.

By 1912, more than 200 Filipino *pensionados* had enrolled in American colleges or universities such as Harvard, Stanford, Cornell, the University of California, Berkeley, and the University of Washington. The pensionados founded Filipino student organizations and college newspapers, some of which are still active today. Then, most returned home to take up leadership roles in the Philippines. Their successes inspired other young Filipinos to seek an education in the United States, with or without scholarships. By the 1930s, about 500 pensionados and 14,000 other Filipino students had attended colleges or universities in the United States.

Most of these students were single young men who settled in university towns. Many supported themselves by working as bellhops, dishwashers, domestic servants, waiters, cooks, housepainters, or laborers. In 1924, more than 100 students got nighttime jobs in the Chicago Post Office as letter sorters. Unfortunately, many would-be students ran out of money and ended up working permanently in very low-paying jobs on West Coast farms and Alaska canneries.

SAKADAS IN HAWAII

Before 1893, Hawaii was an independent kingdom. A few Filipinos had come to Hawaii on Spanish galleons or on whaling ships that docked in Honolulu during the winter. In the mid-1800s, however, American businesses began to move into Hawaii to develop the sugar industry. By 1880, a few American corporations controlled the entire Hawaiian economy. These companies owned thousands of acres of plantation lands and hired thousands of workers. In 1893, American business owners successfully overthrew the queen of Hawaii, Liliuokalani, and, in 1899, after the Spanish-American War, the United States officially took over the country.

Until 1900, American corporations had used Chinese and Japanese workers in the sugarfields, because many native Hawaiians were dying from disease. Beginning in 1906, the Hawaii Sugar Planters Association (HSPA) began to hire Filipinos to fill the shrinking supply of Hawaiian workers and to replace Japanese and Chinese workers. Because Filipino laborers were technically "Americans," U.S. corporations had fewer problems bringing them to Hawaii. The Filipinos called themselves *sakadas*, which in Tagalog means "contract workers." The HSPA signed a contract agreeing to pay the workers' transportation to Hawaii and back to the Philippines and to provide housing for a period of about three years. In many cases, Filipinos stayed on in Hawaii after the contract expired.

The sakada system resulted in a wave of Filipino immigrants to the sugar and pineapple fields of Hawaii. Between 1906 and 1935, about 125,000 Filipino sakadas were brought to Hawaii to work the sugarcane plantations there. By 1925, the HSPA no longer had to recruit in the Philippines; instead, Filipinos showed up voluntarily at the HSPA office in Manila. Most Filipinas (Filipino women), however, refused to emigrate. They felt that traveling to Hawaii and living on plantations was not respectable. By 1920, the ratio of Filipino men to women in Hawaii was about 20 to 1.

Plantation life in Hawaii was very difficult. The backbreaking work included hoeing, weeding, cutting, loading, and hauling. A workday usually lasted from sunrise to sunset. The pay was low and the housing was not good. One former worker remembered,

So hoe hoe hoe is what we did for hours in a straight line and no talking, resting only to sharpen the blade and then walk to the next lot. Hoe every weed along the way to your three rows. Hoe—chop chop chop, one chop for one small weed, two for all big ones. . . . So hoe hoe hoe is what we did until the siren blew at 11:00 sharp for lunch. . . . After one week of hoe hana [work], I felt as if I had been kicked and beaten all over. My body was tight and my back ached . . . that was the first time in my life that I had stooped and worked at one thing for so long without a say and without fun mixed in.[6]

STOOP LABOR

In 1924, the U.S. Congress passed a new immigration bill. The Asian Exclusion Act of 1924 eliminated Chinese, Japanese, and Korean immigration to the United States. The new law did not affect Filipinos, though, because they were nationals and traveled with U.S. passports. They could not be excluded by any legal means.

Because of the new law, in the 1920s, Filipinos became the fastest growing Asian population in the United States. Up and down the West Coast and in Hawaii and Alaska, they took the place of the barred Chinese and Japanese workers on railroads, in canneries, on farms and fields, and in houses. In 1910, only 406 Filipinos lived outside Hawaii; the state of Washington had 17 and California had only 5. Between 1910 and 1930, however, about 50,000 Filipinos arrived on the mainland of the United States. Like the sakadas in Hawaii, these Filipinos were overwhelmingly male (94 percent in 1930). Most of the "Pinoys," as they called themselves, hoped to return to their villages or send enough money back home to buy land.

Agriculture was California's largest industry. It often required 10-hour days of backbreaking work, known as *stoop labor*. Filipino and Mexican workers bent down all day to plant, hoe, or harvest fields of asparagus, lettuce, peas, celery, cauliflower, beets,

In 1924, Congress passed the Asian Exclusion Act, which banned Chinese, Japanese, and Korean immigration to the United States. The law, however, did not apply to Filipinos, who were U.S. nationals, and as a result, they filled jobs previously held by other Asian groups. Many Filipinos, such as these farmworkers in California's Imperial Valley, harvested crops such as lettuce when they worked on these farms.

tomatoes, or spinach. Most of the Filipinos worked on large farms in the San Joaquin, Imperial, Sacramento, and Salinas valleys. American farmers paid Pinoys even less than the Chinese and Japanese for doing the same job, sometimes less than $2 a day. They lived in shacks, tents, or below-standard rooms, and lacked any sort of traditional family life. Farmers often took advantage of Filipino workers, who usually had no way to fight back. They also faced prejudice and violence from native-born Americans. Signs reading "No Filipinos Wanted" were common throughout California.

ALASKEROS

The U.S. territory of Alaska was the third-largest population center for Filipinos behind Hawaii and California. In 1909, Alaska salmon canneries hired recruiters in California to try to persuade Filipinos to move to Alaska. In 1910, more than 200 Filipinos lived in Alaska. These cannery workers called themselves *Alaskeros*.

By the 1920s, many students came to Alaska to work part time in the spring and summer. They earned about $50 a month for working 12-hour days during the 6-month season. They carried the salmon from the boats to the trucks that took them to the canneries. At the cannery, Alaskeros hosed down the fish; sorted them with hooks; cut off their heads and tails; and then cleaned, cooked, canned, and sealed them in cans. Working conditions were cold and unsafe, and living quarters were cramped and unsanitary. Canneries often cheated Filipino workers by taking some of their wages for supposed "living expenses" that were overpriced or never provided at all.

Some Filipino cannery workers married native Alaskan women, and a year-round community began to develop. In 1935, a Filipino community social club formed in Juneau. By 1940, about 9,000 Alaskeros worked in Alaska's canneries.

BY BOAT ACROSS THE PACIFIC

In the early 1900s, Filipinos came to the United States by ship. They usually landed in Honolulu, Seattle, or San Francisco. The journey by ship took about a month. The ship fare from Manila across the Pacific to California was about $70, about two months' wages for an unskilled worker. To many Filipinos, this seemed a small price to pay compared to the potential economic return of a job in America.

The ocean journey from Manila, however, was difficult. Filipinos usually traveled in quarters reserved for the lowest class, with four to six people in a small cabin. Some became sick on the trip. Dolores Quinto remembered, "The boat journey was very trying. The smell of machines and food was enough to make everyone sick. One by one we became seasick for lack of pure air. No one was allowed to go upstairs on deck. Food was placed and served in a great bucket."[7]

Sometimes the hardest part of the trip was the long hours wondering about the future. Filipino-American novelist Carlos Bulosan wrote,

> I found the dark hole of the steerage and lay on my bunk for days without food, seasick and lonely. I was restless at night and many disturbing thoughts came to my mind. Why had I left home? What would I do in America? I looked into the faces of my companions for a comforting answer, but they were as young and bewildered as I, and my only consolation was their proximity and the familiarity of their dialects.[8]

WORKING TOGETHER

When they arrived in America, Filipinos found they had to look out for each other. Like other immigrants, Pinoys often associated with other Pinoys in work and leisure. As early as 1870, Filipinos in Louisiana founded the Spanish-speaking Hispano-Filipino Benevolent Society of New Orleans. This was probably the first Filipino social club in the United States. Wherever large numbers of Filipinos gathered, they usually formed social organizations to help each other, in case of sickness, unemployment, or poverty. Many Pinoys would share living space with several other Filipino men. To some degree, these groups replaced the large close-knit families they had left behind on the islands. In this way, the immigrants made excellent use of the Filipino concept of bayanihan, or cooperative work.

When they were not working, young Pinoys relaxed at pool halls and restaurants opened by Filipino businesspersons. Filipino musical performers, such as Seattle's Moonlight Serenaders, traveled up and down the West Coast entertaining workers. Filipinos frequented dance halls and attended boxing matches. Some read Filipino-American magazines like *The Republic*, published from 1924 to 1933, or *The Filipino Forum*, published in Seattle as the "independent organ of the Filipino community in the Pacific Northwest."

It was only natural that Filipinos should work together to organize labor unions to improve their wages and working conditions. For example, Pablo Manlapit was a sakada who came to Hawaii in 1910. He was so disturbed by agricultural working conditions in Hawaii that, in 1913, he helped establish the Filipino Unemployment Association. In 1919, he started the Filipino Labor Union. Throughout his life, he fought for better conditions for Filipino workers.

In the 1930s, Filipino unions sometimes organized strikes to improve working and living conditions. Thousands of Filipino Americans joined the Filipino Labor Union. Their demands, shocking at the time, do not seem very radical today: 35 cents an hour, an 8-hour work day, employment without considering the race of the worker, and acceptance of the union as a hiring and bargaining agent. Filipino and Mexican agricultural laborers united to gain pay increases and other improvements. The multiracial Filipino Agricultural Laborers Association (FALA), formed in 1938, had 30,000 members in California alone only two years later. Filipinos in the United States were beginning to work together to fight for their rights as Americans.

DISCRIMINATION AND DEPRESSION

Filipinos in the United States faced widespread discrimination and resentment in the 1920s and 1930s. Because they were smaller in stature than most native-born Americans, Pinoys were stereotyped as good for nothing but "stoop labor" or working as "houseboys." They were often denied service in restaurants, movie theaters, swimming pools, barbershops, and bowling alleys. On the mainland, they competed with white

CARLOS BULOSAN: AMERICA IS IN THE HEART

Carlos Bulosan (1913?–1956) was an important Filipino-American writer. Bulosan's most famous work, *America Is in the Heart,* was published in 1946. The book tells the story of the horrible living and working conditions of Filipino immigrants trying desperately to survive in America in the Depression years of the 1930s. Some people consider Carlos Bulosan to be the greatest of all Filipino-American writers.

Bulosan was born in the Philippines in a poor farming village on Luzon. He arrived in Seattle from the Philippines in 1930 at age 17. He had only attended school for three years in the Philippines, spoke little English, and had almost no money. As a result, Bulosan worked the usual jobs for unskilled Pinoy labor. He washed dishes, worked in Alaskan canneries, and picked apples in Washington and fruit and vegetables in California.

As a migrant laborer, Bulosan was shocked to find that living conditions in the United States were worse than those he had left behind in the Philippines. Bulosan found,

> *In many ways it was a crime to be a Filipino in California. I came to know that the public streets were not free to my people: we were stopped each time these vigilant patrolmen saw us driving a car. We were suspect each time we were seen with a white woman.* *

men for jobs and women. Filipino workers faced less prejudice in Hawaii and Alaska, where the workforce was multiracial and there were other Asians.

The Filipino men who came to America before 1940 especially had problems because of the absence of Filipina women. With nine Filipino men for every Filipina woman in the United States, the men often had relationships with native-born women. This infuriated many white racists. There were already many

He later wrote, "I know deep down in my heart that I am an exile in America. I feel like a criminal running away from a crime I did not commit. And this crime is that I am a Filipino in America."**

Bulosan became involved in the labor movement and worked to organize unions to protect Filipino workers. During a long period of poor health, Bulosan read the works of many American writers. This inspired him to write poetry, short stories, essays, and novels. He died in Seattle, poor and unknown, in 1956. In the 1970s, his works were rediscovered by the Asian-American community.

Bulosan struggled to hold on to his faith in the American ideals of democracy and justice that he had been taught in the Philippines. In *America Is in the Heart*, Bulosan attempted to remind Americans to live up to those ideals. He wrote, "America is not bound by geographical latitudes. America is not merely a land or an institution. America is in the hearts of men that died for freedom; it is also in the eyes of men that are building a new world."***

---

 * Available online at *http://college.hmco.com/english/lauter/health/4e/ students/author_pages/contemporary/bulosan_ca.html*

 ** Available online at *http://www.historylink.org/essays/output.cfm?file _id=5202*

*** Available online at *http://www.bulosan.org/html/in_his_words.html*

During the 1920s and 1930s, many Filipino musicians traveled throughout the West Coast entertaining audiences with their blend of Eastern and Western music. Pictured here are the Filipino Serenaders in 1925, with ukuleles, guitars, and mandolins.

laws, known as *antimiscegenation* laws, which prevented "white" people from marrying "black" people. During this time, California, Idaho, Nevada, and Oregon all passed laws prohibiting

Filipinos from marrying "white Americans." U.S. Congressman Richard Welch of California actually told Filipinos that if they did not like it in the United States, they should go home to "join your wives and families, marry into your own race and not with the whites, which is permitted unfortunately in some states of the Union."[9] Amazingly, the U.S. Supreme Court did not declare antimiscegenation laws unconstitutional until 1967.

In some cases, Filipino men were beaten and driven out of town by mobs if they were seen with white women. In 1929, a riot broke out between whites and Filipinos in the farming community of Exeter, California. It ended with a white mob entering a Filipino labor camp and burning down the entire housing complex. Another explosive incident occurred in 1930, near Watsonville, California. Residents complained about "little brown men . . . strutting like peacocks and endeavoring to attract the eyes of young American and Mexican girls."[10] Four hundred whites attacked the Northern Monterey Filipino Club, injuring many Filipinos and killing Fermin Tobera, a farm laborer. The rioting continued for five days. In Los Angeles, more than 1,000 Filipinos marched to protest the death. Other anti-Filipino riots occurred in California—in Salinas (1934) and Lake County (1939). Filipino laborers also faced racism and prejudice in the state of Washington. In 1927 and 1928, mobs forced hundreds of Pinoys to flee the lower Yakima Valley. In central Washington, white ranchers who employed Filipinos faced threats of lynching.

The situation became worse after 1929, when the U.S. economy collapsed. For the next 10 years, jobs were scarce for everybody. This period, known as the Great Depression, was trying for all Americans but especially difficult for minorities. Filipinos were usually part of the first group to be fired, and many could not find work. Native-born Americans blamed immigrants for taking their jobs. For example, San Francisco Judge Sylvain Lazarus commented in 1936, "It is a dreadful thing when these Filipinos, scarcely more than savages, come to San Francisco, work for practically nothing, and obtain the society of these girls. Because they work for nothing, decent white boys cannot get jobs."[11] Because Filipinos in the United States were not citizens, they were not entitled to social services such as unemployment insurance, social security, or public relief.

As the U.S. economy worsened in the 1930s, Pinoys faced even greater discrimination and violence. Filipino attempts to form labor unions in California created tensions with native-born whites. Some Filipino farmworkers in Salinas wrote President Franklin Roosevelt to tell him,

> We find ourselves accused by the general public of lowering the wage scale by working for lower wages and yet forced by the growers to accept a lower scale than corresponding white labor. With the alternative of being subject to mob violence, the destruction of our homes by fire and to unwarranted arrest, if any action is taken to unite for the purpose of maintaining a higher wage scale.[12]

During the 1930s, anti-Filipino sentiment throughout the United States was strong. Several attempts in Congress to limit immigration failed until the passage of the Tydings-McDuffie Act of 1934. This act ended almost 40 years of open Filipino immigration to the United States.

• Study Questions •

1. Why did *pensionados* come to the United States?

2. Who were the *sakadas*?

3. Why did the Asian Exclusion Act of 1924 affect Filipino immigration?

4. Who were the *Alaskeros*?
....

5. Who was Carlos Bulosan?
....

6. What kinds of discrimination did Filipino immigrants encounter in the United States in the 1920s and 1930s?
....

4

New Opportunities

In the United States, the Great Depression of the 1930s led white Americans to fear they would lose their jobs, if they had not already lost them. In addition, Japan's invasion of China worried many Americans. They thought that the ownership of the Philippines would draw the United States into a war in Asia. The U.S. Congress tried to deal with both these worries when it passed the Tydings-McDuffie Act in 1934.

The law immediately changed the Filipino immigrants' status from "nationals" to "aliens." Before 1934, Filipinos could come to the United States in unlimited numbers. By changing the status of Filipinos to aliens, the Tydings-McDuffie Act reduced Filipino immigration to only 50 people per year. The limit on Filipino immigration was supposed to reduce the competition for jobs in the United States. Unfortunately, it meant that Filipino workers in America had almost no chance of ever bringing their families to the United States.

Some Filipinos, faced with discrimination and a crumbling economy, no longer wanted to stay in the United States. They were unable to find work, denied social services available to American citizens, and upset by American racism. Various Filipino groups in the United States began to talk about Pinoys returning to the Philippines. This was called *repatriation*. In 1935, the U.S. Congress passed the Filipino Repatriation Act. The law offered Filipinos free passage back to the Philippines if they wanted to return to their homeland. They would be subject to the 50-person immigration limit, however, if they decided to reenter the United States.

By 1940, about 2,200 Filipinos (of about 45,000) had returned to the Philippines, at an average cost to the U.S. government of $116 per person. By that year, the Filipino population in Washington State had dipped to 2,200 from 3,500 the decade before. In Hawaii, 53,000 Filipinos lived there in 1940, 16 percent fewer than in 1930. Most Filipinos chose to remain in the United States, however.

The Tydings-McDuffie Act also promised independence to the Philippines in 10 years. The U.S. Congress hoped that by distancing itself from the Philippines, the United States would avoid being caught up in an Asian war. They did not realize they were mistaken, however, until Japanese bombers appeared over Hawaii and the Philippines on December 7–8, 1941.

WORLD WAR II

When the Japanese invaded the Philippines, Filipinos and Filipino Americans rushed to join the military. They were eager to defend their homeland. The Filipino men who fought with the Americans in the Philippines took an oath of allegiance to the United States as if they had enlisted in the U.S. Army. By the end of World War II, more than 200,000 native Filipinos had fought against the Japanese in the Pacific Theater. Probably more than 100,000 Filipino soldiers and civilians died in the war.

During World War II, Filipinos fought alongside U.S. troops to protect their homeland from Japan. Pictured here is a U.S. Marine sergeant teaching Filipino soldiers how to load a machine gun on Corregidor Island, Philippines. Shortly after this photo was taken, the Japanese captured the island.

When the war started, Filipinos could not technically join the U.S. Army because they were not citizens. Two weeks after the bombing of Pearl Harbor, President Franklin Roosevelt issued a proclamation that gave Filipino Americans the right to serve in the army and work in defense factories. More than 80,000 Filipino Americans volunteered to serve in the U.S. Army in World War II. In 1942, Roosevelt issued another proclamation granting U.S. citizenship to enlistees. This resulted in many new Filipino-American citizens. So many Filipino Americans volunteered that the United States formed several all-Filipino regiments specializing in jungle and island warfare.

The sacrifice of Filipinos and Filipino Americans paid off in the end. Native-born Americans were less likely to discriminate against people who were fighting with them to defend their country. After years of prejudice, native-born Americans recognized the contributions of Filipinos and had a positive change of attitude.

In 1941 and 1943, Washington State and California made it easier for Filipino immigrants to own property. In 1944, American and Philippine troops liberated the Philippines from the Japanese. On July 2, 1946, President Harry S. Truman signed the Filipino Naturalization Bill, which gave Filipinos residing in the United States the right to become citizens. Two days later, the Philippines gained its independence.

As an independent nation, the quota of Philippine immigrants to the United States was doubled. Because this only increased the number from 50 to 100 Filipinos a year, though, it was not a very big change.

WAR BRIDES

Many Filipinas had worked for the resistance against the Japanese during World War II. They spied for the Americans, cared for the wounded, and delivered messages. Dating between Filipinas and American servicemen was common. Many of these relationships were only *hanggang pier* meaning "until the pier only." This meant that romances between Filipinas and Americans would last only until the Americans shipped out.

However, many Filipinas did marry American men. They were known as *war brides*. They were willing to leave behind their life in the Philippines in exchange for a new life with their husbands in the United States.

In December 1945, the U.S. Congress passed the War Brides Act. This permitted Filipino veterans who had served in the

U.S. Armed Forces and married in the Philippines to bring their wives and children to the United States. In 1948, the California Supreme Court ruled that laws forbidding interracial marriages

FILIPINO SAILORS

For centuries, Filipinos had a reputation as excellent sailors. When the Philippines became an American colony, many adventurous Filipinos found that one way to see the world was to join the U.S. Navy. The navy allowed Filipinos to enlist because they were U.S. nationals. They were restricted to the lowest positions, such as cooks, waiters, dishwashers, and servants, however. By the 1920s, about 4,000 Filipinos served in the U.S. Navy.

The navy paid fairly well, but the best part was that those who served for three years were eligible for U.S. citizenship. As citizens, they could purchase property in the United States. Many Filipinos served a full 20 years, retiring from the service with benefits and settling down in navy towns such as San Diego, California or Norfolk, Virginia. Before Philippine independence in 1946, enlisting in the navy was one of the only ways a Filipino could become eligible for U.S. citizenship.

U.S. merchant ships also took advantage of Filipino seamanship. By 1930, more than 7,000 Filipinos had joined the U.S. Merchant Marine. Unfortunately, the Merchant Marine Act of 1936 required that three-quarters of the crew members aboard American cargo, passenger, and fishing ships had to be U.S. citizens. This resulted in the immediate unemployment of 5,000 Filipinos.

By 1970, almost 17,000 Filipinos served in the U.S. Navy. Recruitment of Filipinos into the navy ended in the 1990s, when the United States agreed to abandon its military bases in the Philippines. Filipinos can still serve in the U.S. military through special programs for the foreign born. In 2003, Filipinos made up one-quarter of the 69,000 foreign born on active duty with the U.S. Armed Forces.

were unconstitutional. The state would no longer support the antimiscegenation laws that had prevented "white" people from marrying "black" people. (The U.S. Supreme Court declared these laws unconstitutional in 1967.) Between 1945 and 1965, 118,000 Filipinas took advantage of the War Brides Act to join their husbands in the United States.

AN INFLUX OF IMMIGRANTS

Filipino immigrants after World War II were different from the young men of the earlier generation. Instead, because of the War Brides Act, the 100-person quota was filled by the wives, children, and family members of earlier immigrants.

Most new immigrants settled in already established Filipino communities on the West Coast. California's Filipino population more than doubled between 1940 and 1960, rising from about 31,000 to 65,000. The number of Filipino Americans in the United States increased from 99,000 in 1940, to 123,000 in 1950, and to 176,000 in 1960. The addition of women and children began to even out the extreme imbalance between Filipino men and women before the war. By 1963, there were fewer than two Filipino males to every Filipino female. This was a huge improvement from the 20-to-1 ratio of 40 years earlier.

As the Filipino population in the United States increased, new employment opportunities opened up. Before World War II, most Filipino immigrants had been male agricultural workers who were restricted from other employment. In many states, the law forbade them from even owning property. In the 1950s and 1960s, the new Filipino immigrants found jobs as clerks and accountants, as well as in the aircraft, electronics, and chemical industries. The Civil Rights Act of 1948 helped lift racial barriers in government jobs. Private businesses began to hire Filipinos. In 1954, Hawaiians elected Peter Aduja to the Hawaii Territorial House of Representatives; he was the first Filipino American elected to office.

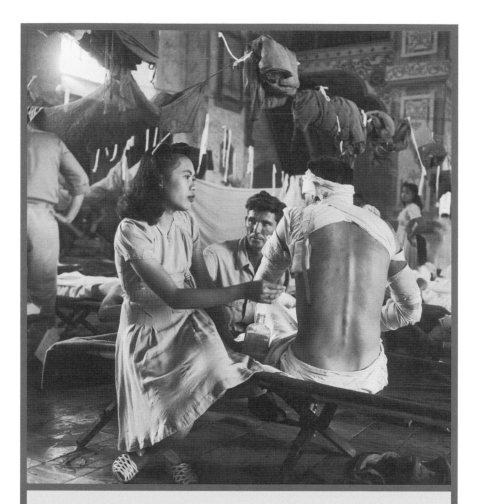

Relationships between U.S. servicemen and Filipina women were common during World War II and sometimes resulted in marriage. The War Brides Act, which Congress passed in 1946, made it legal for U.S. servicemen to bring their Filipino wives and families to the United States. Pictured here is a Filipina nurse taking care of a U.S. soldier during the war.

In 1948, President Truman abolished racial discrimination in the U.S. Armed Forces. Filipinos were now no longer restricted to the lowest positions in the U.S. Navy. By the mid-1980s, more than 400 officers of Filipino ancestry had served in the U.S. Navy.

Although many Filipinos still worked as domestic servants, as kitchen help, or in agriculture, the number was decreasing. In 1950, more than one out of every two Filipinos workers in California were agricultural laborers. Ten years later, it was down to one out of every three. Times were changing.

THE IMMIGRATION AND NATURALIZATION SERVICES ACT

Since the 1920s, there had been a quota (limit) on the number of immigrants allowed into the United States. The quota was based on the country the immigrant came from (country of origin). American immigration law intentionally favored European immigrants over Asian or Hispanic immigrants. When the Tydings-McDuffie Act of 1934 promised independence to the Philippines, Filipino immigrants lost their special status as "nationals." They became subject to the same quotas as other Asians (not counting those Filipinos covered by the War Brides Act).

In 1965, the U.S. Congress changed 40 years of immigration policy by passing the Immigration and Naturalization Services Act. This law abolished the old national origins quota system. Every independent nation outside the Western Hemisphere was able to send up to 20,000 immigrants to the United States a year. The law also ranked immigrants based on their desirability. The United States gave preference to relatives of U.S. citizens and permanent resident aliens (for the reunification of families) and also to persons with special occupational skills, abilities, or training needed in the United States.

This new immigration law was one of the most important acts of Congress in American history. It inspired large numbers of immigrants from the Caribbean, Latin America, and Asia, including the Philippines, to come to the United States. From 1965 to 1985, four times as many Asians settled in the United States as in the entire previous history of the nation. By 2000, more than 10 million Asians lived in the United States—almost

4 percent of the population. More than 1 out of every 10 residents of California, the most populated state in the nation, was Asian-born or of Asian ancestry.

ACROSS THE PACIFIC BY AIR

For Filipinos, the change in the yearly quota from 100 to 20,000 was astounding, and they took full advantage of the new law. Between 1965 and 1985, more than 400,000 Filipinos came to make new homes in the United States. Filipinos especially benefited, because the new law favored the entry of relatives of those already in the United States, and many Filipinos already lived in the country.

In addition, the law encouraged the immigration of professionals such as doctors, lawyers, engineers, nurses, pharmacists, and scientists. Because the Philippines had an education system that made professional training widely available, the ability of Filipinos to acquire employment-based visas was better than immigrants from most other countries. The Philippine educational system was similar to that of the United States, and many Filipinos spoke English, yet there were more college graduates than jobs in the Philippines. After 1965, thousands of educated and highly skilled professionals left the Philippines for the United States.

For many immigrants, the Los Angeles and New York international airports (LAX and JFK, respectively) became the new ports of entry. In 1954, the government closed Ellis Island, the old immigrant center in New York harbor, and turned it into a tourist attraction. The new immigrants from Asia came by airplane, not by boat. One middle-class Filipino immigrant recalled,

> In 1976, when my wife and I arrived here, we disembarked from a Pan Am plane in Honolulu, Hawaii. . . . My first impulse was that I saw in my imagination images of American soldiers during the war, when we used to greet them,

"Hello, Joe!" "Hello, Joe!" "Victory, Joe!" Moreover, I felt we were like herds of cattle to be branded when we were in line to be documented as immigrants to America. It was really a strange feeling in a strange new land.[13]

Filipinos came to the United States for many different reasons: to study, to join their families, to marry, to make more money, or for political reasons. In 2006, there were more than 2 million people of Philippine descent in the United States, and the new wave of immigration shows no sign of slowing down.

• Study Questions •

1. How did the Tydings-McDuffie Act of 1934 affect the Philippines and Filipino immigration?

2. Did most Filipinos in the United States support the Filipino Repatriation Act of 1935?

3. How did the War Brides Act affect Filipino immigration to the United States?

4. Why was the Immigration and Naturalization Services Act of 1965 a huge change in U.S. immigration policy?

5. How did the Immigration and Naturalization Services Act of 1965 affect Filipino immigration to the United States?

6. How many native Filipinos fought against the Japanese in World War II?

5

The Invisible Immigrants

Although there is much to love about the culture and natural beauty of the Philippines, many Filipinos are attracted by the strong economy and English-speaking environment of the United States. According to the 2000 U.S. census, Mexicans were the largest immigrant group, followed by Filipinos, and then Indians, Chinese, and Vietnamese. There were at least 1.4 million foreign-born people from the Philippines in the United States, and more than 2 million Americans identified their ancestry as Filipino. Of the 31 million foreign-born people in the United States in 2000, about 4 percent were immigrants from the Philippines.

In 2000, almost three out of every four Filipino immigrants in the United States lived in five states: California, Hawaii, New York, New Jersey, and Illinois. Almost half of all Filipino Americans lived in California. Because their large numbers in California were still barely noticeable against the enormous population of the state, Filipinos developed a reputation as "invisible immigrants."

In 2000, the 10 states with the largest number of Filipino immigrants were as follows:

State	# of Filipinos	Percent of Total Filipino Immigrants*
California	665,000	49%
Hawaii	102,000	8%
New York	72,000	5%
New Jersey	70,000	5%
Illinois	67,000	5%
Washington	47,000	3%
Texas	46,000	3%
Florida	43,000	3%
Virginia	36,000	3%
Nevada	31,000	2%

*Source: http://www.census.gov

In 2000, Philippine-born immigrants made up less than 1 percent of the total U.S. population. The states with the highest proportion of foreign-born Filipinos in their total populations were Hawaii (8.4 percent), California (2 percent), Nevada (1.6 percent), and Alaska (1.4 percent). In three states, Filipinos made up more than 5 percent of the total foreign-born population: Hawaii (48 percent), Alaska (24 percent), and Nevada (10 percent).

THE PULL OF JOBS

In the Philippines, teachers in public schools were paid about $200 a month. They could make twice as much as domestic helpers in Hong Kong. Government doctors in the Philippines earned around $500 a month, but in North America, a nurse could earn $4,000 a month, or more. In addition, unemployment in the Philippines was usually above 10 percent. With

Many domestic workers emigrate from the Philippines in search of higher wages. Among the more popular destinations is Hong Kong, which is home to some 140,000 Filipinos, many of whom are domestic workers. Pictured here is a group of Filipino domestic workers during their lunch break in Hong Kong's central business district.

700,000 new college graduates every year, the Filipino economy could not create enough skilled jobs for the graduates. In some years, one-half of the physicians trained in the Philippines immigrated to other countries. Filipinos were in demand in other countries, because they usually could read and write, and many spoke English as a first language.

Some Filipinos working overseas performed unskilled and poorly paid work in the oil-producing nations of the Middle East. Filipino workers helped construct the roads and buildings and supported other development in those countries. At the same time, Filipino migrant workers were also attracted by rapid economic growth in Asian areas such as Hong Kong and

Singapore. Many worked in hospitals and nursing homes or as domestic helpers to fill labor shortages.

The outflow of Filipino workers will probably continue for many years. Temporary work overseas has become an accepted part of the economic system of the Philippines. Most of these overseas Filipino workers were reluctant to leave the country for good, but the pull of a better future was too strong. For example, in 2005, Ferdie Del Rosario planned to quit his job in Manila and immigrate to North America. Although he had a college degree and a good job working for a multinational electronics firm in the Philippines, Del Rosario said he was doing it "for the future of my kids. . . . You can see the situation: There are so many graduates but not enough jobs. In my job, there are college graduates who are just machine operators."[14]

THE PUSH OF CORRUPTION

Like Ferdie Del Rosario, many people now emigrating from the Philippines are not poor. Instead, they are engineers, computer programmers, software developers, doctors, and nurses. Many are willing to leave because they have lost hope in a home country that suffers from slow economic growth, ongoing political turmoil, and widespread corruption and poverty. Since the 1940s, opposing political parties in the Philippines have sometimes threatened and even killed each other's candidates and members. This behavior became especially common in the Ferdinand Marcos era (1965–1986). In those two decades, the government's use of terror and fraud was so great that thousands of well-educated people, such as teachers and journalists, left the country, if they could. Between 1968 and 1975, one-quarter of Filipino immigrants admitted to the United States were health professionals, engineers, lawyers, and accountants. Even since Marcos was overthrown, the Philippines has suffered from corruption, favoritism, and violence.

Many Filipinos are not optimistic about their country's future. A 2002 survey by a Manila-based polling company found that one out of every four Filipino adults said they would "migrate to another country and live there" if given a chance. Professionals or skilled workers were tired of the corruption and the bribery that was common in the Philippines.

Dancer Jojo Lucila said he decided to emigrate when he and his children watched the televised corruption trial of former Philippine President Joseph Estrada in 2000. Lucila's children were more impressed by the skill of the lawyers rather than the fact that the former president was on trial for stealing vast sums of money from his country. Lucila complained that in the Philippines, "You can't tell what are the obvious values. Our system is too disorderly. You don't know whom to trust. We want our kids to have a choice of understanding a better country, [learning] what is right and what should be done."

The "brain drain" (educated people moving elsewhere) has a serious effect on Philippine society, but there is almost no way to keep professional Filipinos from leaving the country. Philippine Labor Secretary Patricia Santo Tomas said, "Well, what can we do about it? Tell me, can I prevent you from leaving? I don't think so."

RAPID INCREASE IN IMMIGRATION BETWEEN 1990 AND 2000

Between 1990 and 2000, the United States witnessed a huge increase in Filipino immigration. In those 10 years, the number of immigrants born in the Philippines who moved to the United States increased from 913,000 to 1,369,000. This 50-percent increase meant that almost half a million additional Filipino-born immigrants lived in America. In seven states, led by Nevada, the foreign-born population from the Philippines more than doubled in size between 1990 and 2000:

Increase in Foreign-Born Filipino Population Between 1990 and 2000	
Nevada	271%
North Carolina	156%
Utah	142%
Arizona	142%
Idaho	117%
Georgia	112%
Indiana	105%

Despite their prior history in America as farmworkers, modern Filipino immigrants are mainly an urban group. Less than 10 percent live in rural areas. About three out of every four Filipino city-dwellers came to the United States since 1980. In 2000, the metropolitan areas with the largest Filipino and Filipino-American populations were as follows:

City	Population
Los Angeles	435,000
San Francisco	379,000
Honolulu	191,000
New York City	62,000

LITTLE MANILAS

Before 1965, many Filipino immigrants and their descendants lived closely together in areas known as Little Manilas, Manila Towns, or Filipino Towns. Like many immigrant groups, Filipinos clustered together both for a sense of community and because of native-born American prejudice against them. These *Little Manilas* were filled with restaurants, stores, and social organizations that provided services and a sense of community for Filipino immigrants.

San Francisco's Manilatown was once home to several thousand Filipino immigrants but gradually disappeared between the 1920s and 1960s. The old Manilatown area, which is now part of the city's financial district, is pictured here from atop the new International Hotel Senior Housing building, which was constructed in 2005.

In the 1960s and 1970s, the U.S. government and private developers knocked down many older buildings in cities. Freeways were built right through urban neighborhoods to allow white people to live in suburbia. Most of the older Little Manilas were destroyed. The historical San Francisco Manilatown slowly disappeared until only the International Hotel at the corner of Kearny and Jackson Streets remained. The International, built in 1907, was a low-cost residential hotel that was home to many Asian Americans and especially a large Filipino population. After a long struggle, the International Hotel was demolished in 1981.

In major cities in 2000, only San Francisco's South of Market and Excelsior districts, and Los Angeles's Historic Filipino Town,

Eagle Rock, and Panorama City districts contained enough Filipinos to still be considered Little Manilas. Several new smaller Little Manilas have developed in California, including neighborhoods in Daly City, near San Francisco, and in Carson and West Covina, near Los Angeles. Little Manilas have recently begun to reform in Seattle, Washington; New York City, New York; Chicago, Illinois; Las Vegas, Nevada; Houston, Texas; Fort Wayne, Indiana; and Portland, Oregon.

Saving Stockton's Little Manila

In 1946, Stockton, California, boasted the largest Filipino community outside the Philippines. Stockton is located on the Stockton Ship Channel, about 75 miles (120 kilometers) east of San Francisco. Immigrants came to this inland port in San Joaquin County for agricultural jobs and the promise of a better life in America. Part of Stockton's downtown, known as Little Manila, catered to Filipino immigrants. From the 1920s to the 1970s, community organizations, social groups, and businesses thrived in the area.

In the 1970s, most of the original buildings in Stockton's Little Manila were destroyed in the name of "urban development." By 2000, this once-lively neighborhood was filled with empty lots, fast-food chains, and gas stations. In that year, the city of Stockton recognized the importance of Filipino Americans by dedicating the Little Manila Historic Site. Many Filipinos and other historic preservation groups worked together to save some of the last remaining buildings from destruction.

INCOME AND SCHOOLING

Most Filipinos in the United States have succeeded in raising their standard of living. The percentage of Filipinos living below the poverty line is the lowest among all Asian groups in the United States. According to the 2000 U.S. census, only 6 percent of the country's Filipinos live in poverty (which was determined to be less than $17,000 for a family of four). Filipinos boast the third-highest median family income, averaging $65,000 per household. (Japanese and Asian Indians finished first and second, respectively.)

Tracing Your Roots

HOW TO UNCOVER
YOUR FAMILY'S PAST

Genealogy is the study of family history. Genealogy helps people and families remember their roots. In this way, the history of Filipino immigrants becomes a natural part of the history of the United States and Canada. As one Filipino-American activist noted, "If your identity has no history, you do not exist."

The best place to start in discovering your own ancestors is your own family. Ask your elders the names of your ancestors or stories from the past. You might want to do an oral history of your family recorded on audio or videotape.

It is much easier to trace your family back to the Philippines if you can find a complete name of a relative and where they lived. Try to find someone who was alive at least 70 years ago, such as a grandparent. It helps to have a date of an important event in that relative's life in the "old country," such as a wedding.

Several different types of records can be used to trace your roots. Census records list family members, ages, occupations, and addresses. Vital records give dates and places of birth, marriage, and death. Old newspapers provide a look into the past with news, advertisements, and sports. These can sometimes be found in a good library or online.

Some books specifically help people trace their Filipino ancestors. These books can be found at your local public library. One example is *Tracing Your Philippine Ancestors* by Lee W. Vance. Another possibility is *The Art of Ancestor Hunting in the Philippines* by Luciano P. R. Santiago.

This is even more impressive when compared to the situation of Filipinos in their homeland. In the Philippines in 2003, the annual per-capita poverty line was only 12,267 pesos (about

---

There are also several Web sites that can be helpful. Web sites come and go, so there are surely more sites than the following examples:

Discover Your Ancestors: Ancestors in the Americas
http://www.cetel.org/discover.html

Cyndi's List of Geneaological Sites on the Internet:
    Asia and the Pacific
http://www.cyndislist.com/asia.htm

Philippines-Filipino Genealogy
http://genealogy.about.com/cs/philippines/

FilipinoGeneaology.com
http://www.pinoy.net/.

If you know that your ancestors came to the United States by ship, you can check out Immigration and Passenger arrivals at the National Archives and Records Administration (see *http://www.archives.gov/genealogy/immigration/index.html.*)

Another place to find old documents is the records of the Immigration and Naturalization Service from 1891 to 1957. These records are organized based on the immigrant's port of entry to the United States. Some of these records can be found online, whereas others can still only be accessed by microfilm (see *http://www.archives.gov/research/guide-fed-records/groups/085.html*).

There are also records of passenger lists for vessels arriving at San Francisco between 1893 and 1953. The first 21 rolls on microfilm give the general index of passengers. The second index, on rolls 22–27, is alphabetical and relates specifically to individuals arriving from the Philippines. Each entry provides the date of arrival and the vessel name. Have fun researching!

$225). However, about 4 million families (23 million Filipinos) could not even reach that income. Probably a quarter of the population of the Philippines is living below the Filipino poverty line.

First-generation Filipino Americans place a great deal of emphasis on education for the next generation. Like many immigrant groups, they view education as a way not only to earn more money but also to assimilate into American society. Filipinos have been extremely successful following this philosophy. In 2005, more than four out of every five Filipinos living in the United States had at least a high school diploma. This is the highest rate for any Asian group in America. Almost half of Filipinos in the United States have graduated from college.

FILIPINOS IN CANADA

Despite its cold climate, Canada has also attracted many immigrants from the tropical Philippines. The first Filipino immigrants came to Canada in the 1930s, but in 1964, there were still fewer than 1,000. In 1965 alone, however, more than 1,500 Filipinos entered Canada. In the 1990s and early 2000s, about 10,000 Filipinos immigrated to Canada each year. Filipinos are the third-largest group of immigrants to Canada, just behind Chinese and Indians.

In 2001, there were 328,000 people of Filipino heritage living in Canada. Nearly half (165,000) lived in the province of Ontario, and most of those in Ontario lived in Toronto (140,000). Another 69,000 people of Filipino heritage lived in the province of British Columbia, and 36,000 in Alberta. Filipinos in Canada were more likely than other immigrant groups to have a university degree, but other Filipinos worked in unskilled positions.

Many middle-class Filipinos still saw Canada as a better option than remaining in the Philippines. One Filipino-Canadian explained,

The Filipino community in the Greater Toronto Area strives to preserve their rich cultural heritage as they build lives here in Canada, thousands of miles from home and in most cases, their families. . . . The best part about being a Filipino Canadian is that we live in a city that allows us to embrace our traditions and celebrates them right along with us![15]

• Study Questions •

1. In 2000, how many Americans identified themselves as being of Filipino ancestry?

2. Most Filipinos live in which two states?

3. Why did Filipinos move to the United States?

4. How does the political situation in the Philippines affect Filipino immigration?

5. What three cities have the largest number of Filipino immigrants?

6. What is a "Little Manila"?

7. Why did Stockton, California, have a large Filipino population in 1945?

8. In 2001, how many people of Filipino heritage lived in Canada?

6

Crossing Boundaries

M any immigrant groups feel insecure in the United States. The first generation of immigrants feel compelled to somehow justify their presence in America. This often leads to long lists of achievements by individual immigrants who moved from one country or another.

With more than 2 million people of Filipino ancestry in the United States, Filipinos have no shortage of achievers. A list of successful or important Filipino Americans would make a book in itself. However, in addition to the story of individual accomplishments, Filipinos as a group have attempted to combine the best of their homeland with the best of American culture. This chapter looks specifically at a few particular areas—nursing, music, military service, food, business, boxing, and theater—in which Filipinos as a group have attempted to cross the boundary between the Philippines and the United States, without losing their identity.

FILIPINO NURSES

The Philippines is the world's largest exporter of nurses to foreign countries. In 2000, the United Nations estimated that approximately 250,000 nurses from the Philippines had moved to countries facing a shortage of nurses. In fact, the worldwide demand for Filipino nurses was so great that the emigration of nurses was weakening the quality of health care in the Philippines.

"What can we say as our nurses leave the country? It is primarily for economic reasons," said the president of the Philippine Nurses Association in 2004. In the Philippines, nurses in government hospitals earn about $200 a month. As mentioned previously, in the United States, the same nurses can earn $3,000 to $4,000 a month. Even though Filipino nurses must pass a licensing exam and other tests to practice in the United States, the high pay draws them by the thousands. A nursing position in America also entitles an immigrant to green cards for their families. Although only 4 percent of American nurses were foreign born in 2004, that number represented 90,000 nurses.[16]

Since the 1960s, U.S. hospitals have desperately needed nurses. Because fewer Americans wanted to take on this difficult job, the United States began importing nurses from foreign countries. When the United States abolished the national origins system of immigration in 1965, Filipinos took advantage of the opportunity. By 1972, the Philippines had already become the world's top exporter of nurses to the United States. From 1966 to 1985, at least 25,000 Filipino nurses migrated to the United States. From 2000 to 2004, another 50,000 Filipino nurses found work in the United States. The labor secretary of the Philippines boasted in 2004 that, "Hospitals in the United States traditionally prefer to hire Filipino nurses and other medical workers."

In 2003, Lolita Compas became the first Filipino-American president of the New York State Nurses Association. Compas earned her degree in nursing from St. Paul College in Manila and immigrated to New York City in 1969. As head of

In the United States, Filipino nurses can earn between 10 and 20 times as much as what they would make in their home country. In addition, foreign nurses working in the United States can often earn their work permits faster and obtain green cards for their families. Pictured here are two nurses in Los Angeles, who are talking to an immigration lawyer about the delayed arrival of their green cards.

the 34,000-member nurses' union, Compas tried to clear up cultural misunderstandings between Filipino and American nurses and helped recruiting agencies that wanted to find more overseas nurses. Compas credited her "strong and close" family for giving her the inspiration she needed to accomplish so much. She remembered, "We were encouraged to become good people, good citizens, and to help others."[17]

CROSSING MUSICAL BOUNDARIES

The Filipino people are famous for their musicians and for the quality of their music. Many Filipino singers and musicians make a living entertaining people in other countries, especially in Asia. Music also plays a big part in Filipino-American culture, from karaoke family parties to Filipino-American Association dances. One musician noted, "Family and closeness is a big part of [Filipino] culture. Parents often make us play instruments. Our parents encourage music."

Like most of Filipino culture, Filipino music blends Eastern and Western influences. Philippine music before Spanish colonization included the use of bronze gongs, bamboo nose flutes, and the Malayan orchestra known as the *gamelan*. Spanish colonizers introduced the guitar and the *zarzuela* (a form of operetta). They also helped create "traditional" Philippine musical forms such as the *kundiman* (a romantic love song sung by a rejected lover) and the *harana* (courtship music in which a man woos a woman by strumming a guitar and singing beneath her window at night).

After the Philippines became an American colony, American influences such as blues, folk, and rock 'n' roll joined older Asian and Spanish forms of music. In the late 1950s, Philippine musicians wrote Tagalog lyrics for American rock music. This musical crossing of boundaries was known as "Pinoy rock." In the 1970s and 1980s, Pinoy rock became the music of Filipino protestors against the Marcos government. Punk, grunge, hip-hop, and reggae music all spread from the United States to the Philippines and then returned, slightly changed, with the waves of Filipino immigrants.

Opera singer Evelyn Mandac represents another form of crossing musical boundaries. Mandac, a Philippine native from Bukidnon, is a lyric soprano recognized around the world for her dramatic singing. From 1970 to 1980, Mandac assumed one of the lead roles in more than 20 operas staged at the Metropolitan Opera, in New York City, and appeared in major opera houses in the United States and Europe. She was the first Filipino to sing at the Metropolitan Opera and the Kennedy Center for the Performing Arts in Washington, D.C.

FILIPINO-AMERICAN BUSINESSPERSONS

In general, Filipino Americans are not as committed to entrepreneurship as are other Asian-American groups, such as the Koreans and the Chinese. In the United States, Filipino

---

FILIPINO DJs

Since about 1990, Filipino Americans have been major supporters of rap music. The role of Filipino Americans in shaping hip-hop culture was demonstrated by their skill as DJs. Famous DJs in the 1990s and early 2000s included Rhettmatic, Babu, Symphony, Apollo, Q-Bert, Icy Ice, MixMaster Mike, and Kuttin Kandy. There have been Filipino bedroom DJs who spun in their bedroom as a hobby, mobile house-party DJs who played at parties, and professional DJs who played music on the radio and nightclubs.

In California, Filipino Americans play a crucial role in hip-hop culture. DJ Apollo, one of the most famous and innovative DJs, said that for Filipino Americans growing up in the 1980s in California, DJing was

> . . . the biggest thing. It was, at least that I knew, what the Filipino community did for activities as far as fun. I mean, everybody had a DJ group, and there were parties all over the Bay Area every week. It was a place for the kids to go, for us to DJ. We would do them anywhere we could.*

One Filipino-American guitarist noted in 2004, "A lot of Filipino culture is defined through hip-hop, which is kind of different from other Asians in America. . . . When we grew up, it was all hip-hop."**

---

* Oliver Wang, "Mobile Madness." Available online at *http://sfbg.com/noise/01-01/fili.html*

** Dan Strachota, "Immigrant Songs," August 21, 2002. Available online at *http://www.sfweekly.com/issues/2002-08-21/music/music.html*

businesses mostly appeal to the Filipino-American *kabayan* (compatriots) market; these include small stores, restaurants, cargo shippers, and money remittance centers. Filipino-American businesses tend to start small and remain small. There is some truth to the stereotype that Filipino Americans are not adventurous risk-takers. Because Filipinos can speak and understand English easily, they can usually find a job somewhere in the United States, even if they lack skills. Filipino Americans do not feel the same need that some other immigrant groups feel to take a chance and to go into business for themselves.

Diosdado Banatao

Despite the small number of high-profile Filipino-American entrepreneurs in the United States, there are some noteworthy businesspeople who have made their mark. For example, Diosdado "Dado" Banatao is a well-known entrepreneur and engineer in Silicon Valley, California's high-tech center. Born in 1943, Banatao grew up in the northern part of Luzon. His father was a farmer, and his house had no running water or electricity. Despite his modest beginning, Dado succeeded in getting a degree in electrical engineering and computer science from Mapua Institute of Technology in the Philippines, then Stanford University in California. In 1981, Banatao discovered a way to eliminate big computer chip boards and put the Ethernet controller on a single chip. This controller chip made it much easier to link computers. Banatao also developed advanced computer chip sets that lowered the cost of personal computers and at the same time improved performance. Banatao's new chip-set design produced 10 times more computer power at a thousandth the cost. Many computers' graphics accelerators still use his design.

Loida Nicolas Lewis

Loida Nicolas Lewis is a well-known Filipino-American businesswoman. Lewis graduated from the University of the Philippines College of Law and was the first Asian woman to pass the New York State bar exam without having studied law in the United States. She worked as a lawyer for the Immigration and Naturalization Service from 1979 to 1988. She also wrote three books on American immigration law, including the very popular *How to Get a Green Card.* Lewis became the head of TLC Beatrice in 1994 after her husband's sudden death. Beatrice is a large multinational food company. She moved quickly and successfully to cut costs, reduce debt, strengthen her management team, and sell off parts of the business for a profit. Lewis has also been extremely active in Filipino-American community organizations.

Johnny Valdes

Johnny Valdes, president of Johnny Air Cargo, was working in the Philippines as an accountant when he went to the United States in 1974 on an employee exchange program. He soon realized that Filipino Americans desired many products and services that were not available in the United States. Valdes started his own business selling food products that catered to Filipino Americans. He also traveled back to the Philippines frequently. At that time, postal service in the Philippines was not reliable. Packages required several weeks to reach their destinations, and many disappeared completely. Valdes's friends constantly asked him to carry balikbayan boxes stuffed with goods for relatives to different parts of the Philippines. By 1984, he was carrying so many balikbayan boxes that he created the Johnny Air Cargo Corporation to provide door-to-door freight service between the Philippines and the United States. At first, Valdes operated the business from his home with only two employees. As the Filipino-American population grew, however, business boomed. By 2005, the company had 170 employees and 40 service locations worldwide.

ADVANCING THROUGH THE
U.S. ARMED FORCES

The U.S. military, especially the navy, has been an important source of employment for young Filipinos since the days when the Philippines were an American colony. Many Filipino Americans have risen to high ranks in the U.S. Armed Forces. For example, in 2000, President Bill Clinton appointed Eleanor "Connie" Mariano to the rank of rear admiral, the highest military position occupied by a Filipino-American woman. At the ceremony, Mariano related,

> The Navy meant many things to my family. It meant freedom from poverty, for my father's family was very poor. The Navy meant opportunity to succeed. The Navy meant hope that one day your children would get an education and perhaps boldly dream of becoming doctors or naval officers. The Navy meant all the good things America had to offer.[18]

Some individual Filipino Americans have demonstrated great integrity in their military careers. In 2004, Major General Antonio Taguba became famous throughout the world when he wrote a biting 53-page report on cases of torture at Abu Ghraib, an American prison in Iraq. At Abu Ghraib, American soldiers tortured and humiliated Iraqi prisoners with the implied support of the U.S. Army. Taguba was born in Sampaloc, Manila, in 1950. He learned about the horrors of military abuse firsthand from his father, Tomas Taguba, who survived the Bataan Death March and a Japanese POW prison camp. At age 11, Taguba's family moved to Hawaii. He graduated from Idaho State University with a degree in history in 1972. He then worked his way up through the army, serving in the United States as well as in South Korea, Germany, and Kuwait. In 1997, Taguba became the second Filipino American to attain the rank of general in the U.S. Army. Taguba's report on prisoner abuse at the Abu

Antonio Taguba is only the second Filipino American to attain the rank of major general in the U.S. Army. Taguba earned acclaim in 2004, when he submitted a classified report that revealed U.S. soldiers were torturing Iraqi prisoners at Abu Ghraib prison.

Ghraib prison detailed widespread American crimes "and grave breaches of international law." Taguba was deeply committed to the U.S. Army, but he also believed people should take personal responsibility in matters of right and wrong. A director of the National Military Family Association stated, "He cares deeply about doing the right thing, and it always showed."[19]

FILIPINO-AMERICAN FOOD

Filipino food is often at the center of Filipino-American life. Like many immigrant groups, Filipino Americans use ethnic food as a way to remind them of their homeland. In addition to eating Filipino food at home, there are more than 400 Filipino restaurants in the United States and about 10 more in Canada.

Filipino-American food blends influences from China, Spain, Mexico, and the United States. Native dishes such as grilled shrimp or pork and vegetables in a broth soured with tamarind (a fruit) are still popular. From the Chinese, Filipinos learned the use of soybeans in making sauces and curds, certain ways to prepare pork and beef, and dishes such as spring rolls (*lumpia*), filled buns (*siopao*), and dumplings (*siomai*). *Pancit,* a noodle dish, can always be found at birthday parties, because noodles represent a long and healthy life in Filipino culture.

The Spanish colonists brought to Philippine culture *paella,* a dish made by combining pork, chicken, seafood, ham, sausages, and vegetables. Spanish food for celebrations, like *morcon* (beef rolls), *embutido* (pork rolls), and fish *escabeche,* were taken up by Filipino festival goers. The *lechon,* a spit-roasted pig, is the centerpiece of many Filipino-American celebrations. Filipino deserts such as *leche flan* (caramel custard) show a great deal of Spanish influence, but Filipino Americans also enjoy tropical fruits like coconuts and guavas in syrup.

From Americans, Filipinos learned about foods of speed and convenience for people on the go. Filipino Americans often find themselves eating these kinds of food because of work schedules, especially those who work as caregivers in hospitals. This makes it difficult for people to find the time to cook at home. American salads, cakes, and pies have also become very popular. Yet no matter what they eat, many Filipino Americans try to keep the tradition that the entire meal is placed before the diners at one time. In this way, they are given a choice of all the dishes, whether soup, meat, or vegetables, rather than eating "courses" common in the modern European-American tradition.

Some Filipino Americans have made a career out of producing delicious food. For example, Cristeta Comerford, appointed executive chef at the White House in 2005, was born in Manila in 1962. She was the child of a school principal and a dressmaker, and attended a branch of the University of the Philippines in Quezon City. She left school to immigrate to the

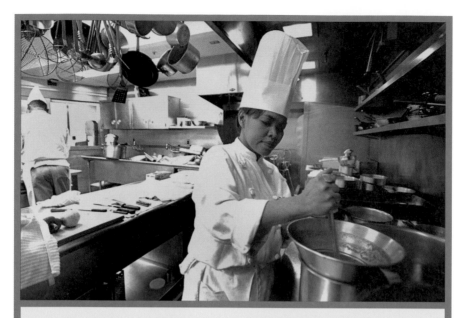

In August 2005, Cristeta Comerford was named the White House's first woman executive chef. Comerford received her bachelor's degree in food technology from the University of the Philippines and previously worked at restaurants in Vienna, Austria, and Washington, D.C.

United States at age 23. Comerford worked at several hotels in Chicago and then as a chef in two restaurants in Washington, D.C. In 1995, she was recruited to work as an assistant chef in the White House. Ten years later, Comerford became the first female executive chef and the first Filipina to hold this position. Laura Bush, the wife of President George W. Bush, said, "Her passion for cooking can be tasted in every bite of her delicious creations."

HAWAIIAN PUNCH

The national sport of the Philippines is *sipa*, which means "kick" in Tagalog. Sipa is played by two to four people who pass a small rattan ball, shuttlecock, or footbag back and forth. The object of the game is to prevent the footbag from touching the ground. A player mainly uses the feet but can use any part of the body except the hands and arms. The game has become popular in the United States, where both the footbag and the game are known as "hacky sack."

Billiards, basketball, and soccer are also popular among Filipino Americans. A billiard table, basketball court, and soccer field can be found wherever Filipinos live in the United States. Of course, individual Filipino Americans have excelled in a wide range of sports. In 1948, Vicki Draves became the first woman to win both the springboard and platform diving titles in the same Olympic Games. Roman Gabriel, a quarterback in American football, was designated Most Valuable Player of the National Football League in 1969, when he played for the Los Angeles Rams. Tai Babilonia, with Randy Gardner, was a five-time national pairs figure-skating champion, and the pair won the world championship in 1979.

Boxing, however, remains a Filipino and Filipino-American specialty and passion. Many Filipino Americans enjoy watching boxing in person or on television. The U.S. military brought the sport to the Philippines in the early 1900s. Matches between soldiers and sailors were popular, and local Filipinos soon picked it up. During the 1920s and 1930s, Filipino men came to the United States not only as farm laborers but also as prizewinning boxers. For example, in 1923, Francisco "Pancho Villa" Guilledo became the world flyweight boxing champion before a packed house in New York City. Villa was an explosive fighter who won 103 of his 108 matches. Other boxers from the colonial period were a source of great pride, unity, and hope for Filipino Americans.

Over the years, more than 30 Filipino and Filipino-American boxers have become world champions, mostly at lighter weight classes. For example, Ben Villaflor, born in 1952 in Negros in the Philippines, moved to Hawaii in 1970 to boost his boxing career. In 1972, Villaflor won the World Boxing Association (WBA) Junior Lightweight Championship (130 pounds, or

59 kilograms) in Honolulu. At age 19, he was the second-youngest boxer ever to win a world boxing title. Villaflor defended his title many times before retiring in 1980 with a record of 44 wins (22 by knockout) and 5 losses. Villaflor liked Honolulu so much that he remained in the city. He eventually became the sergeant-at-arms in charge of providing security for offices and chambers of the Hawaiian Senate.

The Filipino-American boxing tradition continues. In 2005, Brian Viloria, from the town of Narvacan in the Philippines, won the World Boxing Council (WBC) Light Flyweight (108 pounds, or 49 kilograms) Championship. He lived in Hawaii and represented the United States in the 2000 Olympics. Viloria, however, claimed he was a 100 percent Filipino. In his title fight, he had the Philippine flag on his trunks, and, after winning the championship, he wrapped a large Philippine flag around his body. His first comment after winning, while still in the ring, was *"Mabuhay ang Pilipinas!"* ("Long live the Philippines!")

THE MA-YI THEATER COMPANY

The Ma-Yi Theater Company was founded by a group of former University of the Philippines students in 1989. Since then, the company has performed high-quality plays for both Filipino and American audiences. The name *Ma-Yi* comes from the ancient Chinese word for the islands now known as the Philippines. The group began during the political uprisings that swept the Philippines in the final years of the Marcos dictatorship. Ralph Peña, who cofounded Ma-Yi and sometimes serves as its director, said, "We developed a theater company . . . as a way of doing street protests. . . . We got to perform in huge rallies for a million people."[20] When the Office of Army Intelligence called Peña in to question him, he left the Philippines for the United States.

After graduating from the University of California, Los Angeles, Peña moved to New York City. He recalled,

"I'd been working as an actor in New York . . . I got cast as Chinese, and I played a Korean. You never get to play your own ethnicity. Filipinos especially feel that. That got tiring." Peña and some friends decided to start their own theater company. Ma-Yi first produced works staged in the Philippines, but it expanded to perform many new works by Asian-American writers on the immigrant experience. Peña said,

> In the beginning it was strictly looking at the immigrant experience of Filipino Americans. Now, as with a lot of Asian-Americans, the second wave of writers aren't so

JESSICA HAGEDORN: FILIPINO-AMERICAN AUTHOR

Jessica Hagedorn (born in 1949) is no stranger to crossing boundaries. She is a Manila-born poet, performing artist, and writer whose best-selling novels have been published in the United States. As a child in the Philippines, Hagedorn enjoyed American movies, European novels, and radio dramas in Tagalog. Her family moved to San Francisco when she was 14. In that city, she became interested in music, particularly rock, jazz, and rhythm and blues. In the 1970s and 1980s, Hagedorn published several volumes of poetry and performed in musical bands. In the pauses between the songs, Hagedorn performed her own dramatic sketches. She later built on this idea to write multimedia plays.

In 1990, Hagedorn's first novel, *Dogeaters*, became an American best seller. *Dogeaters* mixed together poetry, a gossip column, book and letter excerpts, dramatic dialogue, and news items to tell an angry tale of social injustice set in the Philippines during the corrupt reign of Ferdinand Marcos. On one level, the book was a Filipino American's search for her past and her national identity. Hagedorn has always been interested in writing about the Filipino-American struggle to find or create a place between two cultures.

focused on that particular story. . . . We're looking for plays that have more to say than "I came here and I got lost."[21]

As for his own contribution, Peña wrote *Flipzoids* in 1996. This award-winning play was performed in many cities with large Filipino populations. *Flipzoids* tells the story of three Filipino Americans trying to come to terms with their new identities in the United States. Aying, an elderly Filipina woman, is not sure if she likes living in California. She cannot understand why her daughter, Vangie, is so in love with the United States. Aying spends a great deal of time on the beach. She imagines the Pacific Ocean as a link to her former home, where "stories grow on trees." Vangie is a nurse who loves learning new English words as a way to assimilate into American culture. Like many second-generation immigrants, Vangie is embarrassed that her mother cannot adjust to life in the United States. Through their interactions with Redford, a young Asian-American man who is so completely assimilated that he seems to have no ethnic identity, Peña's characters try to understand what it means to be Filipino, American, or Filipino American. Works like these speak to the Filipino-American community in their quest to cross boundaries without losing an essential part of themselves in the crossing.

• Study Questions •

1. How many Filipino nurses work outside the Philippines?

2. How did the sending of balikbayan boxes lead to a business opportunity?

3. Why did Major General Antonio Taguba become famous?

4. What is *sipa*?

5. Who is Jessica Hagedorn?

6. How does Filipino music represent the merging of many different cultural traditions?

7. How does Filipino food represent the merging of many different cultural traditions?

7

Challenges for the Community

When native-born Americans speak about Asian Americans, they usually are referring to Chinese Americans or Japanese Americans but almost never to Filipino Americans. Many people, including even some residents of the Philippines, consider themselves Pacific Islanders or even Latinos. The Filipino-American community shares this identity crisis. Even as Filipino Americans pass the 2 million mark, their numbers do not always make them stand out in business, media, or culture.

Filipinos are sometimes labeled the "invisible minority" or "invisible immigrants." This is because Filipino immigrants after 1965 seem to have assimilated into American society with relative ease compared to other immigrant groups. Filipino immigrants are usually Christians and speak English fluently. Many are educated and middle class. These characteristics make it easier for Filipinos to fit into American culture.

As one historian noted, however, "You ask a Chinese American or Japanese American who they are and they know. Not so with the Filipinos."[22] Many parents do not teach their children Filipino history and culture. Many younger Filipino Americans do not speak Tagalog, or do not speak it well. The diverse nature of Philippine society further complicates the Filipino identity crisis. With at least eight commonly spoken languages, three distinct geographical divisions, and a 400-year colonial history, it is not clear what "home" or "national" identity means to even those people who live in the Philippines.

Many Filipino-American groups have tried to increase Filipino-American consciousness by promoting the accomplishments and talents of the group. For example, in 2002, Philippine President Gloria Macapagal-Arroyo attended the opening and dedication of the Filipino Community Center in Waipahu, Hawaii. It is the largest institution in the United States with the goal of preserving Filipino-American history and culture and represents only an early step in trying to carve out a more visible Filipino-American identity.

The vagueness of the Filipino and Filipino-American identity extends even to the name they give themselves. Are they "F"ilipinos or "P"ilipinos? Supporters of the use of *Pilipino* argue that using a "P" as a first letter makes a symbolic break from Philippine/Spanish colonial history. After all, the pre-Hispanic alphabet did not even have a letter "F." On the other hand, people who want to use "Filipino" state that members of recent generations, especially in America, have used this name. In the United States, users of "Pilipino" tend to be political activists, whereas users of "Filipino" are more likely to be from earlier groups of immigrants or American-born Filipinos. The debate shows little sign of letting up.

Almost all immigrant groups see at least some of their traditional cultural values weaken over time in a new setting. Filipino Americans have the advantage, at least, of continued

The Filipino Community Center in Waipahu, Hawaii, is the largest such center outside the Philippines. Constructed in 2002, the center serves to preserve Filipino-American history and culture. Pictured here are children from the Filipiniana Dance Troupe in traditional dress during the opening ceremonies for the center on June 11, 2002.

migration between the United States and the Philippines, which keeps cultural ties strong. Other groups, such as Cambodians or Vietnamese, do not experience this continued migration. As one emigrant from the Philippines noted, however, Filipinos "are very good at assimilating into their host societies. Filipinos are quite unique like that."[23] Their adaptability is both an advantage and a disadvantage.

Even those Filipino Americans who enjoy life in the United States sometimes feel homesick. Many miss familiar things they once took for granted, whether Filipino food, music, or a newspaper from the Philippines. Young children might miss the comics and magazines they used to read. Some will even start to miss the Tagalog videos they hardly watched in the Philippines. It is difficult to know which traditions are worth keeping and which can be discarded with little loss.

HOW CUSTOMS DISAPPEAR OVER TIME

One generation is born and lives in the Philippines. Another is born and lives in the United States. In between are the Filipino immigrants who leave one culture to cast in their lot with another. These are the people who often must choose which customs and traditions they will keep and which they will discard. Sometimes the process is quick, but sometimes it is slow and indirect. Below, a Filipino man describes the gradual loss of a Filipino custom:

In the Philippines, when you invite anyone to a restaurant or any eatery, you are expected to pay the bill. Or sometimes, when you are with a group of relatives or friends, you may call the waiter and ask for the bill. As soon as the waiter comes, someone may also try to get the bill. And another may say, "Let me pay! I'll pay!" Or another may try to pull out his wallet from his pocket. This Filipino trait was brought to America by Filipinos from the Philippines.

Later, we abandoned this Filipino practice. It was because there were times, that when it was not your turn to pay, you would not want to order an item that was too costly. So one day, someone suggested, "I think from now on we should pay [for] our own food." Yes, from that day on, we abandoned that Filipino practice, and it was Dutch treat—order what you want and pay for it.*

*Available online at http://www.filipinoamericans.net/lifeinusa.shtml

DUAL CITIZENSHIP

Unlike the wave of immigrants to the United States around 1900, modern-day immigrants often have a much closer relationship with their birth country. The common use of commercial aircraft and the relative inexpensiveness of air travel mean it is now possible for a Filipino American to wake up in Los Angeles and have dinner in Manila.

With so many Filipino workers and immigrants overseas, the Philippine government looked for a way to continue to bind them to their country of birth. In 2003, the Philippine Congress passed a "Citizenship Retention and Re-Acquisition Act." Under this law, Filipino Americans were eligible for dual citizenship in both the United States and the Philippines. This allowed natural-born Filipinos who had become American citizens, as well as their unmarried minor children, to reclaim their Filipino nationality. The law stated that a natural-born Filipino who became a citizen of the United States (or any other country) did not necessarily lose his or her Philippine citizenship. Former natural-born Filipinos who reacquired citizenship could now live in the Philippines continuously without having to apply for an entry visa. They also had the right to travel with a Philippine passport.

One of the main goals of the Dual Citizenship Law was to increase economic growth in the Philippines by convincing overseas Filipinos to return to their homeland and invest their money. The Philippine government assumed that many Filipino Americans, now approaching retirement age, would be more willing to live their retirement in the Philippines if they could lawfully own and invest in Philippine land and businesses.

The results of the Dual Citizenship Law remain to be seen. One older Filipino, however, seemed to think the law would have little effect. He noted:

> At first, many old men or women may plan to go home
> to the Philippines for good. Of course, for them, they

do not want to die in America. Even those who are growing old here at first, want to go back to the old country. . . . With the dollars they saved, and the good exchange currency rate, they can have a happy life in the old country.

. . . When they begin to experience pains in the back and in knees and joints, and the hair continues to turn gray, they normally change their minds. What if they get sick? Medicare cards can't be used in the Philippines. If they have a heart attack in the province, and they plan to go to Manila or to any hospital in a big city . . . they may be declared DOA (dead on arrival). . . . And there's no 911 you can call over there. That's the problem. Later, they decide to stay in their adopted country, the United States. Yes, they will just retire in America. . . . They mention Arizona, Nevada, Florida, South Carolina, and any sunny state in America."[24]

THE FALLOUT FROM SEPTEMBER 11, 2001

Filipino Americans sometimes face discrimination at work. Some businesses have a "bamboo ceiling" that keeps Asians from receiving the highest positions. In general, however, Filipinos do not have to deal with the same sort of prejudice and racism faced by darker-skinned immigrants from areas such as the Caribbean.

Filipinos did have to deal with increased prejudice after the terrorist attacks against the United States in September 2001, however. Abu Sayyaf, a small Philippine Islamic guerrilla group, was linked to the Islamic fundamentalist group al-Qaeda, which was responsible for the attacks on the United States. This placed some Filipino Americans, especially Muslims, under suspicion. Innocent immigrants were sometimes mistreated based on their race and ethnicity.

After 2001, the U.S. government cracked down on foreign visitors and workers living in the United States who failed to meet the requirements of their original visas. The government claimed they did this to protect national security. Many Filipinos had entered the United States on temporary education and work visas but often stayed well past their visa expiration dates. In order to prevent visa fraud, the U.S. Immigration and Naturalization Service was replaced by the U.S. Citizenship and Immigration Services. In this more aggressive atmosphere, there were some cases of unreasonable deportation and visa rejection against Filipino Americans.

The attacks on the United States also affected its relationship with the Philippines. In 2002, President Joseph Estrada signed the Visiting Forces Agreement with the United States. This allowed U.S. soldiers to return to the Philippines, supposedly to fight the "war on terrorism." The U.S. government not only provided training and assistance to Philippine soldiers fighting Islamic guerrillas, but also had U.S. troops participate in joint training with the Philippine military. In 2003, there were nearly 3,000 U.S. soldiers in the Philippines.

YOUTH GANGS

Like young men from many immigrant groups, Filipino teenagers sometimes struggle to adjust to a new country and culture. Sometimes they are attracted by the lifestyle of youth gangs. In general, this is less of an issue for Filipinos than for other Asian groups. Filipinos usually speak some English and have less of a sense of isolation in America than other immigrants. In one poll, however, about a third of Filipino Americans in California reported that Filipino gangs are common where they live. Gang violence has sometimes become a major issue in the Filipino community, especially in the 1980s and 1990s.

For example, Filipino gang members were blamed for drive-by shootings, such as that of Melissa Fernandez in 1994, outside Seattle's Ballard High School. A Filipino rapper in California stated,

I started rapping in the late '80s and early '90s. . . . I wasn't going to break any bones, go to jail or break my wallet from rapping. I was still in Los Angeles back then and the Filipino gang situation was crazy. Rapping and hip-hop offered me an outlet out of that life.[25]

Some Filipinos have banded together to create programs that offer alternatives to gang life. For example, in Seattle, the Filipino community created the Filipino Youth Empowerment Project. The group organizes dances for teenagers, runs a Big Brother/Big Sister program that matches high school students with university students, and created an "Adopt-a-Lolo/Lola" program that allows young people to volunteer time with a grandparent in the community. They also run workshops for

To serve as an alternative to gang life, some Filipino Americans have turned to performing in dance groups. One such group is Los Angeles's Rice Track Family—the first non-African-American group to perform the hip-hop dance known as krumping.

young adults on communication, negotiation, and leadership. In this way, the community attempts to reduce gang-related violence.

Southeast Asian gangs and street cultures were the subject of a special newspaper report by Tomas Alex Tizon, a Pulitzer Prize–winning journalist. Tizon was born in Manila in 1958, but immigrated with his family to the United States at age 4 and grew up in Seattle. Tizon graduated from the University of Oregon and worked for newspapers in Seattle and Los Angeles. Asked of his advice to young journalists, Tizon said, "Read, read, read. Think, think, think. Write, write, write. Go into the dark places and write about them."[26]

DOMESTIC VIOLENCE

Wilson and Felomina Gulen raised three children in Fremont, California, after arriving in the United States from the Philippines in the 1970s. Their relationship grew strained and Felomina eventually filed for divorce. In January 1998, Wilson returned to the house where his wife and mother-in-law were living and shot them both. When police arrived, the 42-year-old Gulen refused to surrender and was killed. These deaths, as well as six others reported among Filipino Americans that year, were all a result of domestic violence.

Domestic violence, also known as family violence, describes a pattern of mistreatment of one person in a family by another person in the family. The mistreatment is often physical, but it can also be sexual abuse, threats, or insults. Women, children, and the elderly are most often the victims of family violence. In the United States, a woman is battered by her husband or boyfriend on the average of every 15 seconds.

Reported incidents of domestic violence seem to be rising in the Filipino-American community. Of seven domestic-violence related homicides in Hawaii in 2000, five of the women killed were of Filipina descent, an unusually high rate considering Filipinos make up only 12 percent of Hawaii's population.

Domestic violence in the Filipino-American community is often not reported, however. Filipino culture generally discourages victims of domestic violence from seeking help. Most Filipinos believe this is something that should be kept within the family, or at least the community. One domestic violence worker stated,

> That is a part of our culture, we don't usually go out and get help. . . . Since we are in this country, nobody wants to listen to us. In the Philippines, it's OK because we have lots of relatives and they're not that busy and they have time to talk. But here everybody is busy and nobody wants to listen because everyone has their own problems.[27]

In response, Filipino Americans have organized workshops on domestic violence and raised funds for the families of victims. They have also formed organizations to combat domestic violence. For example, Filipino American Human Services, Inc. (FAHSI), is a nonprofit organization established in 1993 to provide social services for the poorer individuals of the Filipino community in New York City.

THE MURDER OF JOSEPH ILETO

"Can you mail this letter for me?" a man asked 39-year-old mail carrier Joseph "Jojo" Ileto on August 10, 1999. Ileto took the letter, but as he turned to go, the man took out a handgun from his back pocket and shot the mail carrier nine times. Ileto fell to the ground, face down in a pool of his own blood. The murderer was a white supremacist from Washington State and a member of the hate group Aryan Nations. He killed Ileto several hours after wounding five people at a Jewish community center in Southern California. The killer later said that Ileto was a good person to kill because he was nonwhite and worked for the federal government.

The shooting shocked the Filipino-American community. It reminded Filipinos of the time when white mobs attacked Filipino farmworkers in the 1920s and 1930s. Ileto's uncle said, "instead of us calling him a hero, we should consider his slaying as a wake-up call to all Filipino Americans. We aren't united as a community so we are an easy prey to the bigots among us." In cities throughout the United States, Filipino Americans held protest rallies and marches in memory of Ileto and other victims of hate crimes. They lobbied the U.S. Congress to pass laws giving stricter penalties to those committing hate crimes.

Although hate groups do not single out Filipino Americans any more or less than other Asians, several attacks on Filipinos seem to occur nearly every year. Ileto's family issued a statement saying,

> When Joseph was shot, our entire nation was attacked. America stands for equal justice and freedom for all. We can't allow white supremacists to tear apart our dream. . . . We can only overcome racism and intolerance when we learn to treat each other with respect and dignity. Now is the time for our nation to come together. Celebrate bayanihan.[28]

• Study Questions •

1. Why do Filipino Americans suffer an "identity crisis?"
....

2. Why is assimilating into U.S. society both good and bad for Filipino Americans?
....

3. Why did the Filipino government pass a Dual Citizenship Law in 2003?
....

4. How did the terrorist attacks on the United States in 2001 affect U.S. relations with the Philippines?
....

5. Why is it difficult to help domestic violence victims in the Filipino-American community?
....

6. Why did the murder of Joseph Ileto shock Filipino Americans?
....

8

Politics and Activism

Filipino Americans have made great strides when it comes to improving their earnings in the United States. Filipino-American families tend to have higher incomes than most other immigrant groups. This economic success has not been turned into political power, however. Filipino Americans blend into American society so well that the label "invisible minority" also describes their lack of influence as a group. In the mid-1990s, only about 100 Filipino Americans held elected office, and all but one served at the city or state level.

Traditionally, most Filipino Americans voted for the Democratic Party because of its support for ethnic minority groups and other social issues that affect Filipinos. In the 1990s, however, many Filipino Americans followed other Catholics in a slow movement toward the Republican Party. In 2006, most Filipinos still seem to register to vote as Democrats but only by a slight margin.

A survey of some Filipino-American voters in several states after the 2004 U.S. presidential election revealed that about three-quarters were foreign born and more than a quarter were first-time voters. In that election, Filipino Americans favored the Democratic candidate, John Kerry, over Republican President George W. Bush by a 60 percent to 38 percent margin. When polled, Filipino-American voters expressed concern about the same issues as the voting population in general. However, they also considered issues that pertained specifically to Filipinos, including easing the procedures for the legalization of immigrants, fighting racial profiling, and extending workers' rights.

Filipino Americans also claimed in the survey that they faced voting barriers in the United States. Many complained they were directed to the wrong polling site or had to endure hostile, rude, or poorly trained poll workers. Sometimes Filipinos who by law did not have to provide identification were required by poll workers to provide it, anyway. Filipinos without English-speaking skills had trouble finding Tagalog translators.[29]

FILIPINOS IN POLITICS

A number of individual Filipino Americans have made their mark on the political scene in the United States. Their successes have been greatest in the state of Hawaii and the city of Seattle, Washington. In Hawaii, Benjamin Menor made history in 1974 as the first Filipino American to serve on a U.S. state supreme court. The next year, Kauai residents elected Eduardo Malapit as the first Filipino-American mayor of an American city. In 2000, Robert Bunda was elected president of the Hawaiian State Senate. Romeo (Romy) Munoz Cachola, born in Vigan in the Philippines, was one of the most powerful politicians in Hawaii in the early 2000s. Cachola studied at Quezon University before settling in Honolulu as a real estate agent and entrepreneur. He served in the Hawaii House of Representatives from 1984 to 1992, representing the southern

Robert Bunda, pictured here at the opening session of the Hawaii legislature in January 2004, is the president of the Hawaii State Senate. Bunda is the first Filipino American to serve as president of a state legislature in the United States.

coast of Oahu. He was elected to the Honolulu City Council in 2000 and reelected in 2004.

Filipinos have also been successful in gaining elected office in the Seattle, Washington, area. In 1991, Gene Canque Liddell was elected mayor of Lacey, a suburb of Seattle. She was the first Filipina American mayor. In 2003, David Della, the son of an Ilocano immigrant from Santa Maria, Philippines, won election to the Seattle City Council. At the time, he was the only Filipino American to serve as a city council member of a major American city on the mainland of the United States.

Two other Filipinas have carved out rewarding careers in Washington State politics. Dolores Sibonga was the first Filipina-American lawyer in the state of Washington. In 1978, she became the first member of the Seattle City Council of Filipino ancestry and served until 1990. In 1989, Sibonga ran unsuccessfully for mayor of Seattle. When her political career ended, Sibonga returned to her law practice, served on several state commissions, and wrote for a Filipino-American community newspaper. In 1992, Velma Veloria won election to the Washington State Legislature, to represent the 11th District in Seattle. She introduced legislation to help women and minority businesses. She also organized and led trade missions to Asia; these included a 1994 trip to the Philippines that resulted in the Philippine government opening a trade office in Seattle.

Special notice should also be made of David Mercado Valderrama, who in 1990 became the first Filipino American elected to a state legislature on the mainland United States. He served Prince George's County in Maryland. Robert Cortez Scott, elected to the U.S. House of Representatives in 1992 on the Democratic ticket, was the first African-American Representative from Virginia in more than 100 years. Scott had a grandfather of Filipino ancestry, which also gave him the distinction of being the first American of Filipino heritage to serve in the U.S. Congress.

Filipinos have also achieved some political success in Canada. Arturo Tapiador Viola was born in Santiago, Isabela, and educated as a laboratory technician. He immigrated to Canada in 1967 and became a Canadian citizen in 1973. Viola rose to the position of director of laboratories for an Ontario hospital. From 1994 to 2000, Viola served as mayor of Niagara-on-the-Lake, Ontario, the first Asian of any nationality elected mayor of a Canadian city. Rey Pagtakhan, a doctor and naturalized Canadian citizen, served in the Canadian cabinet from 2001 to 2004. He was the first Filipino Canadian in

BENJAMIN CAYETANO: FROM HUMBLE BEGINNINGS TO THE GOVERNOR'S OFFICE

Benjamin "Ben" Jerome Cayetano served as the governor of the state of Hawaii from 1994 to 2002. As of 2006, this was the highest elected office in the United States ever occupied by a person of Filipino ancestry.

Cayetano was born in Kalihi, Hawaii, in 1939 and raised by his father. As a teenager, Cayetano wanted to be a lawyer, but he recalled, "In that society at that time, it was virtually unthinkable that someone like me could have a shot at it."* Instead, Cayetano worked as a truck driver, apprentice electrician, and metal-packer in a junkyard. In 1963, he moved to Los Angeles and completed two years at Los Angeles Harbor College before transferring to the University of California, Los Angeles (UCLA). He graduated from Loyola Law School in Los Angeles in 1971 and moved back to Hawaii.

Cayetano's public service career began in 1972, when he served on the Hawaii Housing Authority. In 1974, he won a Democratic seat in the State House of Representatives from the Honolulu district of Pearl City and served 12 years in the state legislature. In 1986 and 1990, Cayetano was elected Hawaii's lieutenant governor.

When the governor retired in 1994, the Democratic Party nominated Cayetano to replace him. Cayetano easily won the election and the distinction as the first Filipino-American governor in the United States. In 1998, he won a second term by a single percentage point, the closest election in Hawaii's history. Cayetano left office in 2002, because Hawaiian law did not allow governors to seek a third term. As governor of Hawaii, Cayetano made difficult decisions about taxes and the budget in uncertain economic times. He sponsored the building of schools and state-funded after-school care programs at every public elementary school in Hawaii.

*Available online at *http://www.ucla.edu/spotlight/00/alum_0800_cayetano. html*

Canada's history to be appointed to the cabinet. Pagtakhan was born in Cavite province (south of Manila) in 1935, graduated from the University of the Philippines, and immigrated to the United States to pursue his medical studies. He left the United States for Canada in 1968. He won his first race for a Canadian parliament seat in 1988 and his home district in Winnipeg, Manitoba, reelected him several times.

FILIPINO VETERANS OF WORLD WAR II

Not all of American politics is about individual officeholders. Sometimes, specific issues are of particular concern to a community. The Filipino-American community has concerns that go beyond Filipinos getting elected to office.

For example, during World War II, more than 200,000 Filipinos fought against the Japanese in defense of the Philippines and the United States. Because the Philippines was a colony of the United States before and during the war, these soldiers were technically Americans. To encourage Filipinos to fight, the U.S. government promised them the same health and pension benefits as U.S. soldiers after the war.

During the war, these Filipino recruits shared the same fate as U.S. soldiers in the Pacific Theater. They suffered in the Bataan Death March, survived prisoner-of-war camps, and fought in the countryside as part of the guerrilla resistance, on the battlefields of Luzon and in the Leyte Gulf. President Harry Truman said at the time, "I consider it a moral obligation of the United States to look after the welfare of the Filipino Army veterans."

When World War II ended, however, things were different. In February 1946, the U.S. Congress passed and President Truman signed the Rescission Act. This law said that the service of Filipinos "shall not be deemed to be or to have been service in the military or national forces of the United States or any component thereof or any law of the United States conferring rights, privileges or benefits." This law stripped Filipinos of the benefits they were promised.

The Struggle for Benefits

After 1946, many Filipino veterans traveled to the United States to lobby the U.S. Congress for the benefits promised to them for their service and sacrifice. In 1990, Congress finally passed a new Immigration and Naturalization Act that granted U.S. citizenship to anyone still alive who could prove they had been on active duty in the U.S. Army, the Philippine Army, or the Philippine Scouts during the war. Applicants did not even have to live in the United States. By 1998, about 28,000 Filipino World War II veterans had become U.S. citizens because of this law. These veterans, mostly in their 70s and 80s, received citizenship but were still denied equal status as American veterans. Congress did not want to pay veterans benefits, such as retirement pay, death pay for families, or health insurance, to thousands of elderly World War II veterans, all of whom were past the age of retirement.

Evaristo Edguido was a 79-year-old Filipino former prisoner-of-war who survived the Bataan Death March. He said, "I am alone in San Diego. My family here consists of my fellow Filipino veterans who I live with. I am getting too old. I just want to get my benefits and return to the Philippines, for the last few years of my life."[30] Filipino veterans staged rallies, such as in 1997, when they chained themselves to a statue of General Douglas MacArthur, their former commander, in Los Angeles's MacArthur Park.

Their efforts received a major boost after the terrorist attacks against the United States in September 2001. President George W. Bush wanted to keep strong ties with the Philippines, an important ally in his "war on terrorism." As a reward for Filipino support, the Republican Congress passed a law in 2003 granting full benefits, including long-delayed health benefits and veteran burial rights, to Filipino veterans of the Second World War. The bill affected an estimated 7,000 surviving Filipino World War II veterans living in the United States and cost about $16 million a

Until the passage of the Veterans Benefits Act of 2003, Filipino Americans who served in the U.S. Armed Forces during the Second World War did not receive full benefits from the U.S. government. Prior to this time, these veterans often staged rallies to obtain benefits such as health care and veteran burial rights. Pictured here are two veterans who have chained themselves to the statue of General Douglas MacArthur in MacArthur Park, Los Angeles, to protest the unfair treatment by the U.S. government.

year. After the passage of the health benefits bill, the *Los Angeles Times* included an editorial that stated, "And now, at last, the Filipino veterans are getting their red, white, and blue veterans cards, an honor too long delayed."[31]

ORGANIZING FILIPINO-AMERICAN LABOR

Filipino immigrants who came to the United States before 1965 were stunned when they compared the ideals of the U.S. Constitution, which they had been taught in the islands, with the harsh reality of poverty and American racism. As a result, many

Filipinos worked hard to organize agricultural and cannery workers into labor unions to fight for better pay and working conditions. Filipinos helped organize California grape pickers through the 1950s and 1960s. Their work resulted in the famous grape strike of 1965 and the formation of the United Farm Workers of America (UFW).

Filipino labor organizers also struggled to unionize workers in the salmon canneries in Alaska. In addition, they helped create Cannery Workers Union Local 37, an institution in Seattle's International District for decades. Carlos Bulosan often wrote about the labor-organizing efforts of Filipinos. In *America Is in the Heart*, he expressed his idealism: "America is not a land of one race or one class of men.... We are all Americans who have toiled and suffered and known oppression and defeat, from the first Indian that offered peace in Manhattan to the last Filipino pea pickers."

Avelino "Abba" Ramos worked as a labor organizer for more than 30 years. Born in 1934, Ramos was one of the first children of sugar workers to attend the University of Hawaii. Ramos helped form agricultural unions in Hawaii and then worked as a labor organizer in California from 1962 to 1997. Filipino workers, Ramos said,

> are often still on the bottom. We make the beds. We work in the restaurants, the electronics plants, and the fields. We need to accept the fact we are a working-class community. If we want to advance, we have to unite with other workers like us. That's what we learned in Hawaii.[32]

Filipino Americans have also played a key role in the growing organization of nurses in the United States. In 2000, about 19 percent of the 2.7 million registered nurses in the United States were covered by collective bargaining agreements. One union worker noted,

> In health care, the largest group of minority workers are Filipinos. Unions won't make a dent in organizing the

health care industry without dealing with Filipino workers. That means we have to have a bilingual and bicultural staff, familiar with immigrant issues. We have to understand the social network which already exists in the Filipino community.[33]

The Philippine Nurses Association of America (PNAA) was formed in New Jersey in 1979 to address the issues and concerns of Filipino nurses in the United States. The organization took its current name in 1987. In 2006, the PNAA had 32 chapters across the United States and represented more than 10,000 Filipino-American nurses. Other Filipino organizations, such as the Philippine Nurses Association of New York, are even older. The group was founded in 1929 to speak for Filipino nurses.

THE MURDER OF GENE VIERNES AND SILME DOMINGO

Gene Viernes was born in Yakima, Washington, in 1951. He was the oldest of nine children born to parents who had emigrated from the Philippines to the United States in the 1920s. Gene's father picked fruit and worked in the canneries, and Gene grew up picking fruit before going to school. He spent many summers working in the Alaskan salmon canneries with his father and brothers.

In the 1970s, Gene Viernes became close friends with Silme Domingo. Domingo was born in Texas in 1952. His father left the Philippines in the 1920s, joined the U.S. Army, and fought in the Pacific Theater during World War II. Domingo graduated from the University of Washington and worked to establish social services for poor Filipinos in Seattle. In 1974, Domingo joined the Union of Democratic Filipinos (KDP) and established the Seattle KDP chapter, which organized the first protest in Seattle against the Marcos dictatorship. In 1975, Domingo formed the Alaska Cannery Workers Association as a way to fight racial discrimination in the canneries.

In the 1970s, Filipino seafood processing and cannery workers in Alaska still faced discrimination in obtaining promotions and jobs. They had no upward mobility and lived in bunkhouses that were falling apart. Unfortunately, the old union had become corrupt. It worked with a Filipino gang known as the Tulisan. Union officials forced workers to illegally pay union and gang leaders for the right to be sent to and work in Alaska. The union and the Tulisan organized gambling operations in every Alaskan cannery and workers' bunkhouse. Viernes and Domingo headed a movement to try to better the working conditions for Alaskeros and reform the corrupt union representing cannery workers.

In 1981, Domingo and Viernes were both assassinated inside a downtown Seattle union hall. Philippine dictator Ferdinand Marcos hired the gunmen to murder both Local 37 officers. Their deaths were supposed to prevent any change in the union or challenge to the power of the Tulisan in Alaska. Marcos also hoped it would silence the growing movement in the United States opposing his dictatorship in the Philippines.

Viernes died instantly, but Domingo lived long enough to identify the murderers. The police arrested two cannery workers, who were sentenced to life in prison. A third suspect, Fortunato "Tony" Dictado, leader of the Tulisan, was convicted of ordering the murders, and he, too, was sentenced to life in prison. In a unique ruling in 1989, a U.S. federal court ruled that Ferdinand Marcos had ordered the killings and therefore had to pay a $15 million judgment for his role in the murders.

The killing of Silme Domingo and Gene Viernes horrified the Filipino-American community. Today, the old Local 37 is much better run and provides important services to the Filipino community in Washington and Alaska. It helps with tax returns and sponsors Filipino youth activities. Many other organizations meet in its hall, and the union participates in coalitions on community issues such as immigrant rights.

THE EXPLOITATION OF WOMEN

Another important issue for Filipino Americans outside of electoral politics is the exploitation of Filipino women. Almost 10 percent of the Philippine population works overseas, and more than half of these overseas workers are women. The Philippines is the world's top exporter of women to the international labor market. In some countries, women make up nearly 90 percent of the workers coming from the Philippines.

Many Filipino migrants around the world find themselves abused or exploited by their employers. Women, especially those working in low-paying service industry jobs, are often victims. There are documented cases of Filipino house cleaners who were caned, jailed, burned with a flat iron, made to sleep with the dogs, locked up inside a house, raped, or even murdered. Work in factories is little better than, and sometimes similar, to slavery. One Filipino woman who worked in a textile factory in Taiwan told an interviewer, "It's really very hard; you only have a 15-minute break to eat. . . . They gave me a contract to sign which said you can never have a day off in three years. . . . Never in my wildest dreams would I allow my children to come abroad and work."[34]

Poor Filipino women are particularly victimized by what is known as the *sex trafficking* industry. Sex trafficking is when people are moved from one area to another for sexual purposes. Although many women who leave the Philippines work overseas as domestics (house cleaners, nannies, cooks, etc.), the second-most likely overseas jobs for Filipinas is prostitution. Filipina women are exported under a variety of disguises such as "cultural dancers" or "entertainers." Filipinas are trafficked throughout North America, Asia, Europe, the Middle East, and Africa. Many of these women are deceived by being promised jobs as waitresses or nannies only to discover too late that they are meant to be prostitutes. These prostitutes are almost slaves; they are forced to work and are not free to leave.

Another form of abuse of women is the mail-order bride business. Mail-order bride agencies provide men with names, addresses, telephone numbers, pictures, and other information about women listed in their catalog or on their Web site. The men pay from $50 to $800 for this information. Many Filipinas have ended up trafficked, battered, abused, raped, or murdered in this so-called "marriage." Although many mail-order brides come from Eastern Europe, more than half of the women for sale come from the Philippines. The United States is the top recipient of mail-order brides.

Some Filipino Americans are working to end abuse of Filipino women. Washington State Representative Velma Veloria has taken a special interest in fighting the international sexual

Some Filipino women leave their country to pursue jobs as nannies or waitresses, but, instead, are often forced to become prostitutes. Pictured here is a group of women outside the employment department in Manila protesting plans by Japan to limit the number of visas offered to Filipino women.

trafficking of Filipino women. Ninotchka Rosca, an activist and writer, is spokesperson for the Purple Rose Campaign against the exploitation of Filipino women and children. Rosca was born in Laguna, California, raised in the Philippines, and studied comparative literature at the University of the Philippines. She was a political prisoner under the Marcos regime and left the Philippines in 1982 to live in New York City. She has written several books and is best known for her novel *Twice Blessed*. Rosca helped found the Gabriela Network, the primary women's rights organization in the Philippines.[35]

• Study Questions •

1. Who are two noteworthy Filipino-American politicians?

2. Who are two noteworthy Filipino-Canadian politicians?

3. Why do you think the U.S. government refused to pay benefits to Filipino World War II veterans?

4. Why were labor unions important to Filipino Americans?

5. Why were Gene Viernes and Silme Domingo murdered?

6. Who was Ben Cayetano?

7. How are Filipino immigrant women exploited?

9

An Ongoing Story

Like most immigrant groups in the United States, Filipino Americans are caught between two worlds. Because they have voluntarily moved from the Philippines, they realize full well the shortcomings of their homeland. At the same time, many Filipino immigrants miss the traditions and routines of life back home. They feel uncomfortable with modern life in the United States and its emphasis on individualism, materialism, and "getting ahead." Filipino Americans try to keep traditional values, but adapt them to their new circumstances in the United States. In this way, they hope to create a lifestyle that respects the old ways while looking ahead to a better future.

Every day, hundreds of young Filipinos arrive at the Overseas Employment Administration Office in Manila hoping for a better life. Greg Fernandez, who left the Philippines to work in the hotel industry, said, "They say there is no place like home, but given a chance to work abroad for better pay and better conditions, I don't think anyone would stay in their own country." Fernandez added, however, "Of course we miss our families in the Philippines, but we stay in close contact so even though we live abroad, we still feel very much part of the country."[36]

THE APL SONG

Allen Pineda Lindo, known as "apl.de.ap," captured the Filipino dilemma in a rap song he named "The APL Song." Apl.de.ap was born near Angeles City, in the Philippines, and grew up in Pampanga. He was adopted into an American family in Los Angeles when he was 14, leaving behind his birth family. In 1995, he joined a musical hip-hop group called the Black Eyed Peas. Filipino Americans formed the Black Eyed Peas' first major fan

Allen Pineda Lindo, better known as apl.de.ap, is one of the founding members of the hip-hop group the Black Eyed Peas. Born in Angeles City in the province of Pampanga in the Philipines, apl.de.ap has integrated Tagalog into some of the group's songs, including "The Apl Song," which recounts his life in the Philippines. The Black Eyed Peas are pictured here at the 2005 Grammy Awards (from left to right— Taboo, Fergie, apl.de.ap, and will.i.am).

base. After a couple of moderately successful CDs, in 2003 the Black Eyed Peas recorded *Elephunk*. It became one of the biggest CDs of the year, selling more than 7 million copies worldwide.

As a musician and rapper, apl.de.ap has remained loyal to the Philippines. One of the songs on *Elephunk* was "The APL Song." Many people in the Filipino-American community could relate to "The APL Song" because the song reflects their experience. The first verse describes the pros and cons of apl.de.ap's impoverished life in the Philippines, whereas the second verse talks about his feelings on returning to the Philippines 10 years later. The song was unusual because the chorus is written in Tagalog. In addition, the music video combines the work of many Filipino-American entertainers, such as music producer Chad Hugo and actors Dante Basco and Joy Bisco.

THE OVERSEAS ABSENTEE VOTING ACT OF 2003

There are limits to the Filipino-American desire to be involved with the Philippines, however. In 2003, the Congress of the Philippines passed a law allowing Filipinos who had left the Philippines and migrated elsewhere to vote in the presidential elections. The only condition was that they must promise under oath to return to the Philippines and permanently live there within three years from their registration as absentee voters.

Because about 10 percent of Filipinos live and work overseas, this could have been a huge change in the politics of the Philippines. More than 4 million of the 7 million overseas workers scattered around the world were eligible to vote in the 2004 presidential elections. "This is long overdue," said one newspaper editor. "For as long as I can remember, overseas Filipinos have been clamoring for the right to vote. . . . We are propping up the economy, so it is only right that we should be more involved in domestic politics."[37]

The results of the act, however, were disappointing. The Philippine government originally hoped that 2.5 million overseas Filipinos would vote. This goal was lowered to 1.7 million, then 800,000. In the end, only 354,000 Filipinos even registered to vote. Of this number, 230,000, or 65 percent, voted in the 2004 elections. This was less than 1 percent of all registered voters. Asian and Middle Eastern countries had more overseas voters than American and European countries—Saudi Arabia and Hong Kong had more than half of the total number of Filipino registered overseas voters.

Filipinos in the United States seemed particularly uninterested in voting. In the entire United States, only 3,537 Filipino Americans even registered to vote, out of an estimated 386,000 eligible voters. Of that number, only 1,730, or 49 percent, cast votes in the 2004 Philippine election. Some Filipino Americans lived too far away from the eight Philippine diplomatic centers

Although the Congress of the Philippines passed the Absentee Voting Act in 2003—which gave Filipinos who live in foreign countries the right to vote—voter turnout for the 2004 elections was disappointing. Pictured here are Filipino workers casting their ballots at a Hong Kong voting center on May 9, 2004.

in the United States and could not afford to take time off from work or pay the travel fare. They were also reluctant to pledge to return home within three years. An editorial in a Filipino-American newspaper said, "Unless the law is amended to make it easier for everybody to register and vote by mail, no amount of persuasion can make the majority of the Filipinos in America exercise their right of suffrage."[38]

Some Filipinos expressed disappointment over the low turnout and proposed elimination of the law. For the moment, however, the government of the Philippines decided to leave it on the books. A government representative noted, "Just like births, the first Overseas Absentee Voting exercise was not without pains. But like a child growing up, we know that one

THE HONEST CABDRIVER

On the night of July 14, 2004, 46-year-old Nestor Sulpico was driving his taxicab in New York City when he realized that a passenger had accidentally left a backpack on the back seat. The Filipino cabdriver opened the pack and was stunned to find it filled with black pearls. Sulpico, who was earning $80 a day for a twelve-hour shift, imagined how the jewels, worth about $70,000, could change his life. Later, he said, "I thought of the days when I was just roaming New York, shivering in the snow, desperately looking for a job." Sulpico, however, decided to return the jewels. He commented, "I believe that honesty is the most important virtue, which serves as a foundation of all other virtues."*

When Sulpico was growing up in the Philippines, his idol was José Rizal. Now Sulpico was a sort of modern-day hero. The passenger who left the jewels gave him a small reward and raised several thousand dollars toward an education fund to help Sulpico finish his nursing studies. Sulpico had not returned to the Philippines for 15 years, but he told everyone he was proud to be day, the overseas absentee votes would make a difference in the whole Philippine electoral exercise."[39]

THE SPIRIT OF BAYANIHAN

As of 2006, the Filipino diaspora looked set to continue for many more years. Overseas migration is an effective way to alleviate a labor surplus in the Philippines, keeping unemployment levels in the country under control. At the same time, Filipino immigrants and overseas workers send home vast sums of money that help the Filipino economy.

In 2004, the foreign affairs secretary of the Philippines met with the Filipino community of New York. In his speech to these immigrants and children of immigrants, he summed up

a Filipino. In his honor, the Senate of the Philippines passed a resolution paying tribute to his honesty. It read,

> At a time that often tries the Filipino soul, . . . the singular act of honesty of Mr. Sulpico has raised the Philippines to a [high level of] prestige as a land of dependable and trustworthy people. Mr. Sulpico now stands as a symbol of the Filipino abroad—an Asian who is honest and upright, and one whose character any employer can truly trust and be proud of.**

---

* Nestor Burgos Jr., "Honest Cabbie: I Dreamt of Doing Something Good," *INQ7.net*, July 25, 2004. Available online at *http://www.inq7.net/nat/2004/jul/25/nat_9-1.htm*

** Efren L. Danao, "Pinoy Taxi Driver in New York Commended," *Manila Times*, July 30, 2004. Available online at *http://www.manilatimes.net/national/2004/jul/30/yehey/top_stories/20040730top8.html*

the pride that Filipinos living at home feel about the accomplishments of the ongoing Filipino diaspora:

> You are powerful living symbols of what the Filipino can achieve. . . . Your individual and collective accomplishments will surely serve as a source of pride and inspiration to millions of our countrymen. More importantly, you have put our country on a pedestal, commanding the respect and admiration of other sovereign nations. But what is truly endearing about you is that in spite of your successes, you have not forgotten our motherland. You have remained Filipinos at heart, and in word and in deed. You have not forgotten the bayanihan spirit for which we are known the world over.[40]

Chronology

1521	Spanish expedition led by Ferdinand Magellan lands in the Philippines.
1565	Spanish rule of the Philippines begins.
1571	Spanish found the city of Manila.
1587	First Filipinos in North America land near San Luis Obispo, California.
1763	First permanent Filipino settlements established in North America near Barataria Bay, in southern Louisiana.
1870	Filipinos found the Hispano-Filipino Benevolent Society of New Orleans, probably the first Filipino social club in the United States.
1896	Spanish execute José Rizal in the Philippines.
1898	United States defeats Spain in the Spanish-American War.
1899	U.S. Congress ratifies Treaty of Paris and annexes the Philippines; Philippine revolt against U.S. rule begins.
1903	United States defeats Philippine revolt; U.S. Congress passes Pensionado Act.
1906	Hawaii Sugar Planters Association begins hiring Filipinos as contract laborers.
1909	Alaska salmon canneries begin recruiting Filipinos to work in Alaska.
1910–1930	Filipino laborers migrate to the United States to perform agricultural labor in California and Washington.
1923	Francisco Guilledo wins world flyweight boxing championship in New York.

1924	U.S. Congress passes Asian Exclusion Act.
1925–1940	Filipino labor leaders organize unions to improve working conditions.
1927–1928	White mobs riot against Filipinos in Yakima Valley, Washington.
1929	Great Depression begins in the United States.
1930	Whites attack Filipinos in a riot in Watsonville, California.
1934	U.S. Congress passes the Tydings-McDuffie Act.
1935	U.S. Congress passes Filipino Repatriation Act.
1938	Filipino Agricultural Laborers Association created.

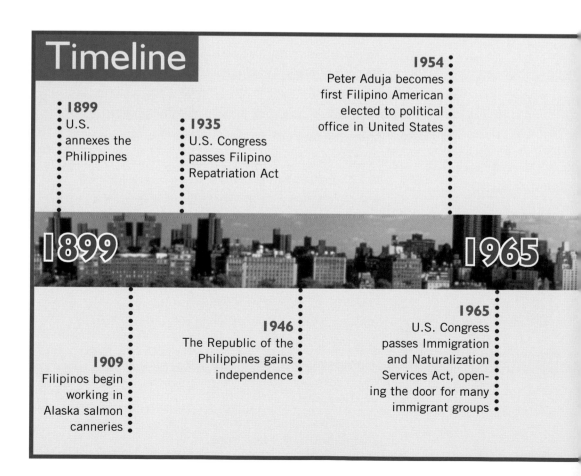

Timeline

1899
U.S. annexes the Philippines

1935
U.S. Congress passes Filipino Repatriation Act

1954
Peter Aduja becomes first Filipino American elected to political office in United States

1899

1965

1909
Filipinos begin working in Alaska salmon canneries

1946
The Republic of the Philippines gains independence

1965
U.S. Congress passes Immigration and Naturalization Services Act, opening the door for many immigrant groups

1941   Japan attacks U.S. and Filipino forces in the
         Philippines; President Franklin Roosevelt issues
         a proclamation that gives Filipino Americans
         the right to serve in the U.S. Army and work in
         defense factories.

1942   Japanese conquer Manila, Bataan, and
         Corregidor.

1944   U.S. and Filipino forces invade the Philippines; U.S.
         Navy crushes the Japanese Navy in the Battle of
         Leyte Gulf.

1945   Manila is liberated; World War II ends.

1946   The Republic of the Philippines becomes inde-
         pendent; U.S. Congress passes Rescission Act;

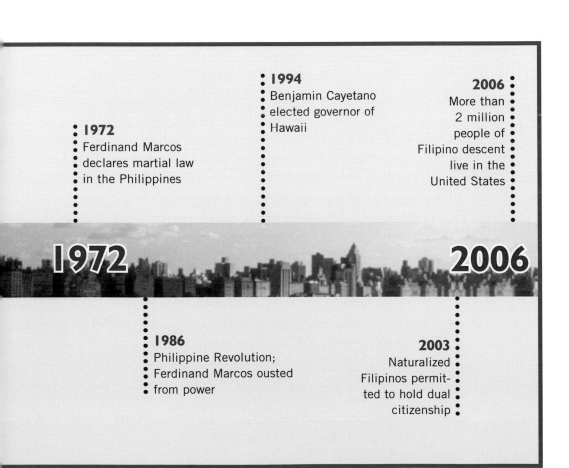

1994
Benjamin Cayetano
elected governor of
Hawaii

2006
More than
2 million
people of
Filipino descent
live in the
United States

1972
Ferdinand Marcos
declares martial law
in the Philippines

1986
Philippine Revolution;
Ferdinand Marcos ousted
from power

2003
Naturalized
Filipinos permit-
ted to hold dual
citizenship

	Carlos Bulosan publishes *America Is in the Heart*; War Brides Act takes effect; Stockton, California, has largest Filipino population outside of the Philippines.
1948	California Supreme Court rules that laws forbidding interracial marriages are unconstitutional.
1950–1965	Filipinos help organize California grape pickers into United Farm Workers of America.
1954	Peter Aduja becomes first Filipino American elected to office as a member of the Hawaii House of Representatives.
1965	U.S. Congress passes Immigration and Naturalization Services Act; Ferdinand Marcos elected president of the Philippines.
1965–1985	More than 400,000 Filipinos move to the United States.
1972	Ferdinand Marcos declares martial law in the Philippines (which lasts until 1981).
1981	Silme Domingo and Gene Viernes assassinated inside a Seattle union hall; International Hotel in San Francisco demolished.
1983	Opposition leader Benigno Aquino assassinated on his return to Philippines.
1986	The Philippine Revolution of 1986 (EDSA Revolution); Cory Aquino becomes president of the Philippines; Ferdinand Marcos flees to the United States, where he dies in exile in 1989.
1989	The Ma-Yi Theater Company founded.
1990	Jessica Hagedorn's novel, *Dogeaters*, becomes a best seller in the United States.
1992	Velma Veloria becomes first Filipino American elected to the Washington State legislature; U.S. closes naval base at Subic Bay and Clark Air Base in the Philippines.
1994	Benjamin Cayetano elected governor of Hawaii; he is the first Filipino-American governor.
1999	Joseph Ileto is murdered by white supremacist.

2001   Joseph Marcelo Estrada is removed from office
        in the Philippines in a revolt known as EDSA
        II; Filipino-Canadian Rey Pagtakhan serves in
        Canadian cabinet until 2004.

2002   Filipino Community Center opens in Waipahu,
        Hawaii.

2003   Philippine Congress allows Filipinos natural-
        ized in the United States to hold dual citizen-
        ship; Philippine Congress passes the Overseas
        Absentee Voting Act.

2006   More than 2 million people of Filipino descent live
        in the United States and 350,000 in Canada;
        about 10 percent of the population of the
        Philippines lives outside the country.

Notes

Chapter 1

1. Joey Alarilla, "Fil-Ams Seek More Clout in US Politics," September 3, 2002. Available online at *http://www.inq7.net/gbl/2002/sep/03/text/gbl_7-1-p.htm*.
2. Ibid.
3. "Anxiety Grips Filipinos Living or Working Abroad," *Asian Political News*, February 28, 2005. Available online at *http://www.findarticles.com/p/articles/mi_m0WDQ/is_2005_Feb_28/ai_n11843955*
4. Alberto G. Romulo (Philippines Foreign Affairs Secretary), "THE FILIPINO, STANDING PROUD IN ANY LAND," remarks during his Meeting with the Filipino Community, Philippine Center, New York, September 28, 2004. Available online at *http://www.dfa.gov.ph/archive/speech/romulo/proud.htm*.

Chapter 2

5. Carl Schurz, "*American Imperialism*, speech delivered at the University of Chicago on January 4, 1899.

Chapter 3

6. H. Brett Melendy, *Asians in America: Filipinos, Koreans, and East Indians* (Boston: Twayne Publishers, 1977), 86.
7. Melendy, 39.
8. Carlos Bulosan, *America Is in the Heart: A Personal History*. Chapter 13 (Seattle: University of Washington Press, 1973), 96.
9. Hyung-chan Kim, *The Filipinos in America, 1898–1974: A Chronology and Fact Book* (Dobbs Ferry, N.Y.: Oceana Publications, 1977), 92.
10. Melendy, 55.
11. Melendy, 47.
12. Kim, 79.

Chapter 4

13. "The Voyage to America." Filipino Americans.Net. Available online at *http://www.filipino-americans.net/voyage_to_america.shtml*.

Chapter 5

14. Mynardo Macaraig, "More Filipinos Brave Canada's Cold Climate to Seek Better Future," *Manila Times*, May 14, 2005. Available online at *http://www.manilatimes.net/national/2005/may/14/yehey/opinion/20050514opi6.html*
15. Judy, "Proud to be Filipino-Canadian!" June 16, 2005. Available online at *http://toronto.metblogs.com/archives/2005/06/proud_to_be_fil.phtml*.

Chapter 6

16. Catherine Ceniza Choy, *Empire of Care: Nursing and Migration in Filipino American History* (Durham, N.C.: Duke University Press, 2003).

17. Diane Pineiro-Zucker, "NYSNA President Lolita Compas: Taking the Helm and Pledging a Commitment to NYSNA's Ideals." New York State Nurses Association, January 2004. Available online at *http://www.nysna.org/departments/communications/publications/report/2004/jan/compas.htm*.

18. Ramon Farolan, "The United States Navy in the Lives of Filipinos," INQ7.net. July 20, 2003. Available online at *http://www.inq7.net/opi/2003/jul/20/opi_rj-farolan-1.htm*.

19. Laura Sullivan and David L. Greene, "Taguba Is Called a Straight Arrow," *Baltimore Sun*, May 6, 2004. Available online at *http://www.baltimoresun.com/news/nationworld/iraq/bal-te.taguba06may06,1,2149169.story?coll=bal-nationworld-utility*

20. "Ma-Yi Theater Company." Available online at *http://www.donshewey.com/theater_articles/ma-yi_theater_company.htm*

21. Ibid.

Chapter 7

22. Quote by Filipino-American historian Fred Cordova, author of *Filipinos: Forgotten Asian Americans*, in K. Connie Kang, "Filipinos Happy with Life in the U.S., but Lack United Voice," *Los Angeles Times*, January 26, 1996. Available online at *http://www.geocities.com/benign0/agr-disagr/3-2-filam.html*

23. Bethan Jinkinson, "Empowering the Philippines' Diaspora," *BBC News-World Edition*, February 13, 2003. Available online at *http://news.bbc.co.uk/2/hi/asia-pacific/2725211.stm*

24. Veltisezar Bautista, "Life in These United States." Available online at *http://www.filipino-americans.net/lifeinusa.shtml*.

25. May Chow, "Hip Hop for Charity VYDC and 'AsianWeek' Team up for APA Heritage Month." Available online at *http://news.asianweek.com/news/view_article.html?article_id=5933526cb88384ec4458fe9514a78a26&this_category_id=171*.

26. "Alex Tizon - Pulitzer Prize." Available online at *http://www.txtmania.com/articles/alex.php*

27. Stacy Lavilla, "Standing up to Domestic Violence: Asian Americans Come Together to Fight a Family Threat," *Asian Week*, March 12–18, 1998. Available online at *http://www.asianweek.com/031298/bay.html*

28. Available online at *http://72.9.242.6/node/291*.

Chapter 8

29. "The Filipino American Vote." Asian American Legal Defense and Education Fund. Available online at *http://www.aaldef.org/images/filipino.pdf*.

30. Roderick Sasis, "Freedom and Justice for All? Filipino American Veterans 'Served but Don't Deserve.'" Web Magazine Online. Available online at *http://www.sscnet.ucla.edu/aasc/classweb/fall97/M163/sasis4.html.*

31. Percy Della, "Headlines that Touched Filipinos in U.S. in 2003," *Global Nation.* Available online at *http://www.inq7.net/globalnation/sec_new/2003/dec/31-01.htm*

32. David Bacon, "The Living Tradition of Filipino Union Activism." Available online at *http://dbacon.igc.org/Phils/06LivingTradition.htm*

33. Ibid.

34. Bethan Jinkinsin, "Empowering the Philippines' Diaspora." BBC News: World Edition, February 13, 2003. Available online at *http://news.bbc.co.uk/2/hi/asia-pacific/2725211.stm.*

35. Gayle Gupit-Mayor, "Ninotchka Rosca." *NW Asian Weekly.* Available online at *http://home.comcast.net/~gayle.mayor/Rosca.htm.*

Chapter 9

36. Bethan Jinkinson, "Empowering the Philippines' Diaspora," BBC News World Edition, February 13, 2003. Available online at *http://news.bbc.co.uk/2/hi/asia-pacific/2725211.stm*

37. Ibid.

38. Jose Katigbak, "Washington Report: Pinoys in U.S. Ho-Hum on Absentee Voting." Available online at *Philippine Headline News Online*, September 12, 2003. Available online at *http://www.newsflash.org/2003/05/ht/ht003727.htm*

39. "Commission on Elections; Republic of the Philippines." Available online at *http://www.comelec.gov.ph/oav/oav.html*

40. Alberto Romulo, "The Filipino, Standing Proud in Any Land," September 28, 2004. Available online at *http://www.dfa.gov.ph/archive/speech/romulo/proud.htm*

Glossary

Alaskeros   Filipinos working in the Alaskan salmon industry.

ama/ina   Filipino word for father/mother.

antimiscegenation laws   U.S. laws that made it illegal for "white" people to marry "black" people; especially common between 1860 and 1960.

assimilate   Fit into a new environment, or the social or cultural tradition of a group.

balikbayan boxes   Boxes stuffed with imported goods sent by Filipino immigrants to relatives and friends back in the Philippines.

barong tagalog   A type of formal menswear of the Philippines.

bayanihan   Helping other people; cooperative work.

colony   A territory ruled by a distant power.

culture   The learned behaviors of a group.

diaspora   Migration or scattering of people from their original homeland, often because of conquest, slavery, or poverty.

EDSA Revolution   Philippine Revolution of 1986; EDSA stands for Epifanio de los Santos Avenue, the main highway in Manila, where Filipinos assembled in a nonviolent mass demonstration against the Marcos government.

Filipino   A person who lives in the Philippines, whether male or female; a woman is sometimes called a Filipina.

Filipino American   A Filipino or Filipina who has come to live in the United States.

genealogy   The study of family history.

Little Manila   An area in which Filipino immigrants and their descendants cluster together; also known as Manila Towns, or Filipino Towns.

lolo/lola   Filipino word for grandfather/grandmother.

Manilamen   Filipino sailors who served on Spanish ships in the 1600s and 1700s.

martial law   A law that places the military, instead of the civilian government and the police, in complete control of a country.

pagmamano   The Philippine custom of taking an older person's right hand and bringing it to their forehead as a sign of respect.

pakikisama   Smooth social interaction; for example, acting pleasantly even if angry.

pensianados   Filipinos college students who came to the United States on U.S. government scholarships provided by the Pensionado Act of 1903.

Pilipino   The Philippine national language (also known as Filipino or Tagalog); also refers to being from the Philippines.

Pinoy   A shortened form of the term *Filipino American*; sometimes used to mean not just being a Filipino by birth but also in thought, deed, and spirit.

remittance   The act of sending money to someone, especially money sent from overseas back to a person's native country.

repatriation   To restore or return, either voluntarily or by force, to the country of one's birth.

sakadas   Filipino contract workers, usually employed in Hawaiian agriculture.

sex trafficking   To carry on the illegal business of moving people from one area to another for sexual purposes.

sipa   The national sport of the Philippines, known in the United States as "hacky sack."

stoop labor   A type of backbreaking labor in agricultural fields, often performed by Filipinos in the United States between 1920 and 1945.

Tagalog   The Philippines national language; also known as Filipino or Pilipino.

utang na loob   A debt of gratitude; if someone does a favor for another person, that person is obligated to return the favor at some future time.

war brides   Women of an area who marry visiting or occupying soldiers; for example, Filipinas who married U.S. servicemen during World War II.

Bibliography

Bandon, Alexandra. *Filipino Americans.* New York: New Discovery Books, 1993.

Bautista, Veltisezar. *The Filipino Americans: From 1763 to the Present.* Farmington Hills, Mich.: Bookhaus, 1998.

Bulosan, Carlos. *America Is in the Heart: A Personal History.* Seattle, Wash.: University of Washington Press, 1973.

Bryan, Nichol. *Filipino Americans.* Edina, Minn.: ABDO Publishing, 2003.

Cordova, Fred. *Filipinos, Forgotten Asian-Americans: A Pictorial History.* Dubuque, Iowa: Hunt, 1963.

Espiritu, Yen Le. *Filipino American Lives.* Philadelphia, Pa.: Temple University Press, 1995.

————. *Home Bound: Filipino American Lives Across Cultures, Communities, and Countries.* Berkeley: University of California Press, 2003.

Fujita-Rony, Dorothy. *American Workers, Colonial Power: Philippine Seattle and the Transpacific West, 1919–1941.* Berkeley: University of California Press, 2002.

Posadas, Barbara. *The Filipino Americans.* Westport, Conn.: Greenwood, 1999.

Root, Maria. *Filipino Americans.* Thousand Oaks, Calif.: Sage, 2004.

WEB SITES

Where Immigrants Live: An Examination of State Residency of the Foreign Born by Country of Origin in 1990 and 2000
http://www.cis.org/articles/2003/back1203.html.

Filipinos in Canada, Ryerson School of Journalism: Diversity Watch
http://www.diversitywatch.ryerson.ca/backgrounds/filipino.htm

Filipino-American Literature
http://www.english.emory.edu/Bahri/Filipino.html

The Filipino Americans: Yesterday and Today
http://www.filipino-americans.com/cgi-bin/redirect.cgi?url=yes_today.html.

Filipino Americans.Net
http://www.filipinoamericans.net/

White Supremicist Ordered to Pay Maximum Penalty for Hate Crime Slaying
http://forums.yellowworld.org/archive/index.php/t-13136.html.

Filipinos Happy with Life in U.S., But Lack United Voice
http://www.geocities.com/benign0/agr-disagr/3-2-filam.html

Fil-Ams Seek More Clout in US Politics
http://www.inq7.net/gbl/2002/sep/03/gbl_7-1.htm.

Filipinos Have Lowest Poverty Rate Among Asians In U.S.
http://inquirer.stanford.edu/Fall2004/bend1/Filipinos.html.

Filipino-American Literature
http://www.literaryhistory.com/20thC/Groups/Filipino.htm.

More Filipinos Brave Canada's Cold Climate to Seek Better Future
http://www.manilatimes.net/national/2005/may/14/yehey/opinion/20050514opi6.html.

The Foreign Born from the Philippines in the United States
http://www.migrationinformation.org/USfocus/display.cfm?id=179.

Americans of Filipino Descent—FAQs
http://www.personal.anderson.ucla.edu/eloisa.borah/filfaqs.htm

Looking Backwards, Looking Forwards, PUSOD: Philippines–U.S.
http://www.pusod-us.org/events/dmartinez.html

Filipino-American Resources
http://www.seattleu.edu/lemlib/web_archives/Filipino/history.html.

Profile of the Foreign-Born Population of the United States: 2000
http://72.14.207.104/search?q=cache:fgOawZYDLp8J:www.census gov/prod/2002pubs/p23-206.pdf+census+2000+nationality+ immigration&hl=en&ie=UTF-8.

Further Reading

Bandon, Alexandra. *Filipino Americans.* New York: New Discovery Books, 1993.

Bartell, Karen. *Fine Filipino Food.* New York: Hippocrene Books, 2003.

Bautista, Veltisezar. *The Filipino Americans: From 1763 to the Present.* Farmington Hills, Mich.: Bookhaus, 1998.

Langellier, John. *Uncle Sam's Little Wars: The Spanish-American War, Philippine Insurrection, and Boxer Rebellion, 1898–1902.* Philadelphia, Pa.: Chelsea House, 2002.

Stern, Jennifer. *The Filipino Americans.* New York: Chelsea House, 1989.

Winter, Frank. *The Filipinos in America.* Minneapolis, Minn.: Lerner, 1988.

WEB SITES

Filipino-American Literature
http://www.english.emory.edu/Bahri/Filipino.html

Filipino Americans.Net
http://www.filipinoamericans.net/

The Filipino Americans: Yesterday and Today
http://www.filipino-americans.com/cgi-bin/redirect.cgi?url=yes_today
html

Fil-Ams Seek More Clout in US Politics
http://www.inq7.net/gbl/2002/sep/03/gbl_7-1.htm

Filipino-American Literature
http://www.literaryhistory.com/20thC/Groups/Filipino.htm.

The Foreign Born from the Philippines in the United States
http://www.migrationinformation.org/USfocus/display.cfm?id=179

Filipino-American Resources
http://www.seattleu.edu/lemlib/web_archives/Filipino/history.html.

Picture Credits

Index

A

Abu Ghraib, Iraq, 83–84
Adopt-a-Lolo/Lola, 99
Aduja, Peter, 59
agriculture
    in California, 43–45
    in Hawaii, 41–43
    labor unions and, 47
Aguinaldo, Emilio, 26, 28
Alaska
    canneries, 45, 112, 113–114
    racial discrimination in, 49
Alaskeros, 45, 114
alien status, 40–41, 54
America Is in the Heart (Bulosan), 48–49,
    112
anti-imperialists, 28
antimiscegenation laws, 50–51, 58–59
"APL Song, The," 120
apl.de.ap, 119–120
Aquino, Benigno, Jr., 33
Aquino, Corazón, 33–34
Arab traders, 24
Asian Exclusion Act (1924), 43
assimilation
    desire for, 19
    difficulties of, 118
    education and, 74
    literature and, 89
    preserving identity and, 11–12
    success of, 92

B

Babilonia, Tai, 87
balikbayan boxes, 13, 82
bamboo ceiling, 97
Banatao, Diosdado "Dado," 81
barong tagalog, 11
Bataan Death March, 30
Battle of Leyte Gulf, 31
Battle of Manila Bay, 26
bayanihan, 16, 123–124
benevolent societies, 46–47
boxing, 87–88

Bulosan, Carlos, 46, 48–49, 112
Bush, George W., 105, 110
Bush, Laura, 86
business success, 80–82, 97

C

Cachola, Romeo (Romy) Munoz, 105–106
California
    agriculture in, 43–45, 61
    Asians in, 62
    Filipino population after World War
        II, 59, 64–65
    Filipino population in 1900, 43
    hip-hop culture, 80
    labor unions in, 47, 112
    Little Manilas, 70–71
    marriage laws in, 50–51, 58–59
    property ownership in, 57
    racial discrimination in, 45, 48, 51
Canada, 74–75, 107, 109
cannery workers, 45
Cannery Workers Union, 112, 113, 114
Cayctano, Benjamin "Ben" Jerome, 108
China, 23–24
Christians, 22, 24, 92
citizenship
    dual, 96–97
    military service and, 56–57, 58
    status as nationals and, 40–41
    for World War II veterans, 110
Citizenship Retention and Re-Acquisition
    Act (2003), 96–97
Civil Rights Act (1948), 59
Clark Air Base, 32, 34
Clinton, Bill, 83
clothing, 11
Cojuangco, Mariá Corazón "Cory"
    Sumulong. *See* Aquino, Corazón
Comerford, Cristeta, 85–86
commonwealth status, 29
Compas, Lolita, 77–78
computer chips, 81
contract workers, 42
cooperative work, 16
Cuba, 26–27

"cultural dancers," 115
culture
  continuing immigration to maintain,
    93–94, 95
  described, 11, 15–17
  disappearance of, 95
  food, 84–85
  influences on, 22
  music, 79
customs. *See* culture

D

debts of gratitude, 16, 17, 37
Del Rosario, Ferdie, 67
Della, David, 106
Democratic Party, 104–105
deportations, 98
Dewey, George, 26
diaspora, 13–14
Dictado, Fortunato "Tony," 114
discrimination. *See* racial discrimination
DJs, 80
Dogeaters (Hagedorn), 89
domestic violence, 100–101
Domingo, Silme, 113–114
Draves, Vicki, 87
dual citizenship, 96–97

E

Edguido, Evaristo, 110
education, 41, 74
elders, respect for, 11, 17
Elephunk, 120
English language skills
  assimilation and, 92
  employment and, 62, 66
  reason for, 23
Epifanio de los Santos Avenue. *See* ESDA
  Revolution
EDSA II, 35
EDSA Revolution, 33–34
Estrada, Joseph Marcelo, 34–35, 68, 98
ethnicity, 21–22, 23–24

F

family
  immigration and reunification of,
    61, 62
  importance of, 17, 19
  studying history of, 72–73
  violence in, 100–101
favors, 16, 17, 37
Fernandez, Greg, 118–119
Fernandez, Melissa, 98

Filipino Agricultural Laborers Association
  (FALA), 47
Filipino American Human Services, Inc.,
  101
Filipino Cajuns, 40
Filipino Community Center, 93
Filipino Creoles, 40
Filipino Forum, The, (magazine), 47
Filipino Labor Union, 47
Filipino League, 25
Filipino Naturalization Act (1946), 57
Filipino Repatriation Act (1935), 55
Filipino Towns, 69–71
Filipino Unemployment Association, 47
Filipino Youth Empowerment Project,
  99–100
Filipinos/Filipinas, 13–14
Flipzoids (Peña), 90
food, 84–86

G

Gabriel, Roman, 87
Gabriela Network, 117
gangs, 98–100, 114
genealogy, 72–73
Great Depression, 29, 51–52, 54
Guilledo, Francisco "Pancho Villa," 87
Gulen, Felomina, 100
Gulen, Wilson, 100

H

"hacky sack," 87
Hagedorn, Jessica, 89
hanggang pier relationships, 57
Hawaii
  Filipino population in 1900, 43
  Filipinos as percent of population,
    100
  labor unions in, 47, 112
  political power in, 59, 105–106, 108
  racial discrimination in, 49
  sakadas, 41–43
Hawaii Sugar Planters Association (HSPA),
  42
hip-hop culture, 80, 119–120
Hispano-Filipino Benevolent Society of
  New Orleans, 46
houseboys, 48
How to Get a Green Card (Lewis), 82

I

Idaho, 50–51
identity
  crisis, 93

ethnicity, 21–22, 23
in literature, 89
preserving, 11–12
racial, 92
Ileto, Joseph "Jojo," 101–102
immigration
after World War II, 59, 64–65, 68–69
dual citizenship and, 96–97
early, 39–41
encouraged by Philippine
government, 13
to Hawaii, 41–43
maintaining culture by continued,
93–94, 95
of nurses, 77
Philippine independence and, 57
quotas, 61
reasons for, 15, 64–68, 118–119
status, 40–41, 54
via airplane, 62–63
via ships, 45–46
Immigration and Naturalization Act
(1990), 110
Immigration and Naturalization Services
Act (1965), 61
income, 71–74, 77, 104
International Hotel (San Francisco,
California), 70
interracial marriage, 50–51, 58–59
invisible immigrants, 64–65, 92

J

Japan, 29–31, 55–57
jobs
DJs, 80
exploitation of women, 115–117
immigration and, 65–67
labor unions and, 47, 111 114
migrant laborers, 48
nurses, 77–78, 112–113
racial discrimination and, 48–49,
51–52, 59
Johnny Air Cargo Corporation, 82

K

kabayans, 81
Katipunan, 25
Kerry, John, 105

L

labor unions, 47, 111–114
languages, 11, 23
Lapu Lapu (chief), 24
Lazarus, Sylvain, 51–52

Lewis, Loida Nicolas, 81–82
Liddell, Gene Canque, 106
Lindo, Allen Pineda, 119–120
literature, 25, 89, 112
Little Manilas, 69–71
Los Angeles, California, 70–71
Los Angeles Times (newspaper), 111
losing face, 16
Louisiana, 40, 46
Lucila, Jojo, 68
Luzon Indians, 39

M

Ma-Yi Theater Company, 88–90
Macapagal-Arroyo, Gloria, 35, 37, 93
MacArthur, Douglas, 29–30, 31
Magellan, Ferdinand, 24
mail-order brides, 116
Majapahit, 23
Malapit, Eduardo, 105
Malay people, 23
Mandac, Evelyn, 79
Manila, Philippines
founded, 24
importance of, 21, 23
trade and, 24–25
Manila Towns, 69–71
Manilamen, 40
Manlapit, 47
Marcos, Ferdinand
Domingo and Viernes murders and,
113, 114
Philippines under, 32–34, 67
protesters against, 15
Mariano, Eleanor "Connie," 83
marriage, 50–51, 57–59
martial law, 32–33
McKinley, William, 26
Menor, Benjamin, 105
Merchant Marine Act (1936), 58
migrant laborers, 48
missionaries, 24
Moonlight Serenaders, 47
music
early traveling performers, 47
hip-hop, 80, 119–120
influences on, 78–79
Muslims, 22, 97

N

national status
Asians excluded and, 43
citizenship and, 40–41
ended, 54
Nevada, 50–51

Noli Me Tangere (Rizal), 25
nursing, 77–79, 112–113

O

Oregon, 50–51
Overseas Absentee Voting Act (2003),
     120–123
overseas Filipinos, 13–14, 66–67, 115–117

P

pagmamano, 11
Pagtakhan, Rey, 107, 109
pakikisama, 16
pancit, 85
Peña, Ralph, 88–90
Pensionado Act (1903), 41
People Power Revolution. *See* EDSA
     Revolution
personal relationships
     benevolent societies and, 46–47
     family, 17, 19
     hanggang pier, 57
     importance of, 16–17
     romantic, 49–51, 57–59
Philip II (king of Spain), 24
Philippine-American War, 28–29
Philippine Nurses Association of America
     (PNAA), 113
Philippine Republic (Japanese), 30–31
Philippine Revolution of 1986. *See* EDSA
     Revolution
Philippines
     absentee overseas voting, 120–123
     American military bases, 32, 34, 58
     brain drain, 68
     economy, 13–14, 65–66, 73–74, 96,
          123
     encouraged immigration, 13
     government corruption, 67–68
     health care, 77, 97
     history, early, 23–24
     history after Marcos, 33–35, 37
     history as American colony, 28–31
     history as Spanish colony, 24–27, 39
     history under Marcos, 15, 32–34, 67
     independence, 31, 57
     national sport, 86–87
     overview of, 20–23
     war on terrorism and, 98, 110
Pilipinos, 93
pineapple plantations, 42–43
Pinoy rock, 79
Pinoys, 13
Poe, Fernando, 35
political power

     in Canada, 107, 109
     in Hawaii, 59, 105–106, 108
     party affiliation, 104–105
     in Washington State, 106–107
prejudice. *See* racial discrimination
pride, 16
property ownership, 57, 59
prostitution, 115–117
Purple Rose Campaign, 117

Q

Quinto, Dolores, 46

R

racial discrimination
     after September 11, 2001, 97–98
     in Alaska, 49
     in California, 45, 48, 51
     in Hawaii, 49
     jobs and, 48–49, 51–52, 59
     marriage and, 50–51
     military ended, 60
     military service during World War II
          and, 57
     during 1920s and 1930s, 48–49,
          51–52, 55
     Treaty of Paris and, 28
     violence, 101–102
     voting barriers, 105
     in Washington State, 51
Ramos, Avelino "Abba," 112
Ramos, Fidel, 34
rap music, 80, 119–120
religion, 22, 92, 97
remittances, 13, 123
repatriation, 55
Republic, The (magazine), 47
Republic of the Philippines. *See* Philippines
Republican Party, 104–105
Rescission Act (1946), 109
restaurants, 84
riots, 51
Rizal, José, 25–26
Rodrigues, Antonio Miranda, 40
Roman Catholics, 22
romantic relationships, 49–51, 57–59
Roosevelt, Franklin, 56
Rosca, Ninotchka, 117
Roxas, Manuel, 31

S

sailors, 58
sakadas, 41–43, 47

Salinas, Rodney, 11–12
salmon canneries, 45
San Francisco, California, 70
Santo Tomas, Patricia, 68
Schurz, Carl, 28
Scott, Robert Cortez, 107
self-esteem, 16
September 11, 2001, 97–98
service industry jobs, 115
sex trafficking industry, 115–117
Sibonga, Dolores, 107
sipa, 86–87
social clubs, 46–47
Spain, 24–28, 29, 39–40, 85
Spanish-American War, 26–27, 29
sports, 86–88
Sri Vijaya, 23
standard of living, 71–74
stereotypes, 48
Stockton, California, 71
stoop labor, 48
street culture, 98–100
Subic Bay Naval Base, 32, 34
sugar industry, 41–43
Sulpico, Nestor, 122–123

T

Tagalog, 11, 23
Taguba, Antonio, 83–84
Taguba, Tomas, 83
theater, 88–90
Tizon, Tomas Alex, 100
Toronto, Ontario (Canada), 74–75
Touch Me Not (Rizal), 25
trade, 23–25, 39
Treaty of Paris, 28
Truman, Harry S., 57, 60, 109
Tulisan, 114
Twice Blessed (Rosca), 117
Tydings-McDuffie Act (1934), 29, 54, 55, 61

U

unions, 47, 111–114
United Farm Workers of America (UFW), 112
United States
    Filipino population distribution, 64–65, 68–69
    Filipino population in 1900, 43
    Filipino population in 1940, 55
    foreign-born in, 64
    military bases in Philippines, 32, 34, 58
    Philippine-American War, 28–29

Philippine independence, 31
    Spanish-American War, 26–27, 29
    Supreme Court, 51
    urban development of, 70–71
    war on terrorism, 98, 110
    World War II, 29–31
U.S. Armed Forces
    advancing through, 83–84
    Filipinos currently in, 58
    Filipinos serving during World War II, 31, 55–57, 58
    racial discrimination ended in, 60
    World War II veterans, 109–111
utang na loob, 16, 17, 37

V

Valderrama, David Mercado, 107
Valdes, Johnny, 82
Veloria, Velma, 107, 116–117
Viernes, Gene, 113–114
Vietnam War, 32, 33
Villaflor, Ben, 87–88
Viloria, Brian, 88
Viola, Arturo Tapiador, 107
Visiting Forces Agreement (2002), 98
voting, 105, 120–123

W

war brides, 57–59
War Brides Act (1945), 57–59
war on terrorism, 98, 110
Washington State
    Filipino population in 1900, 43
    political power in, 106–107
    property ownership in, 57
    racial discrimination in, 51
Welch, Richard, 51
women
    activists, 117
    authors, 89
    businesspeople, 81–82
    chefs, 85–86
    exploitation of, 115–117
    government officials, 106, 107, 116–117
    in Navy, 83
    in sports, 87
World War II, 29–31, 55–57, 109–111

Y

youth gangs, 98–100

Z

Zobel, Alan, 15

About the Contributors

Series Editor **Robert D. Johnston** is associate professor and director of the Teaching of History Program in the Department of History at the University of Illinois at Chicago. He is the author of *The Making of America: The History of the United States from 1492 to the Present*, a middle-school textbook that received a *School Library Journal* Best Book of the Year award. He is currently working on a history of vaccine controversies in American history, to be published by Oxford University Press.

Jon Sterngass is the author of *First Resorts: Pursuing Pleasure at Saratoga Springs, Newport, and Coney Island*. He is currently a freelance writer specializing in children's nonfiction books. His most recent work for Chelsea House is a biography of José Martí. Born and raised in Brooklyn, Sterngass has a B.A. in history from Franklin and Marshall College, an M.A. in medieval history from the University of Wisconsin–Milwaukee, and a Ph.D. in American history from City University of New York. He has resided in Saratoga Springs, New York, for 13 years, with his wife, Karen Weltman, and sons Eli (12) and Aaron (9).